TRAVELS WITH GEOFFREY
IF IT CAN GO WRONG, IT WILL

SHARON HAYHURST

Copyright © 2021 Sharon Hayhurst
Cover design by Joe Shepherd www.heyjoeillustration.com

Production and formatting by AntPress.org

First Edition

The author asserts the moral right under the Copyright, Designs and Patents Act 1988 to be identified as the author of this work.

All rights reserved. No part of this publication may be reproduced, stored in a retrieval system, or transmitted, in any form or by any means without the prior written consent of the author, nor be otherwise circulated in any form of binding or cover other than that in which it's published and without a similar condition being imposed on the subsequent purchaser.

Some names, places and other details have been changed to protect the privacy of individuals mentioned in the book.

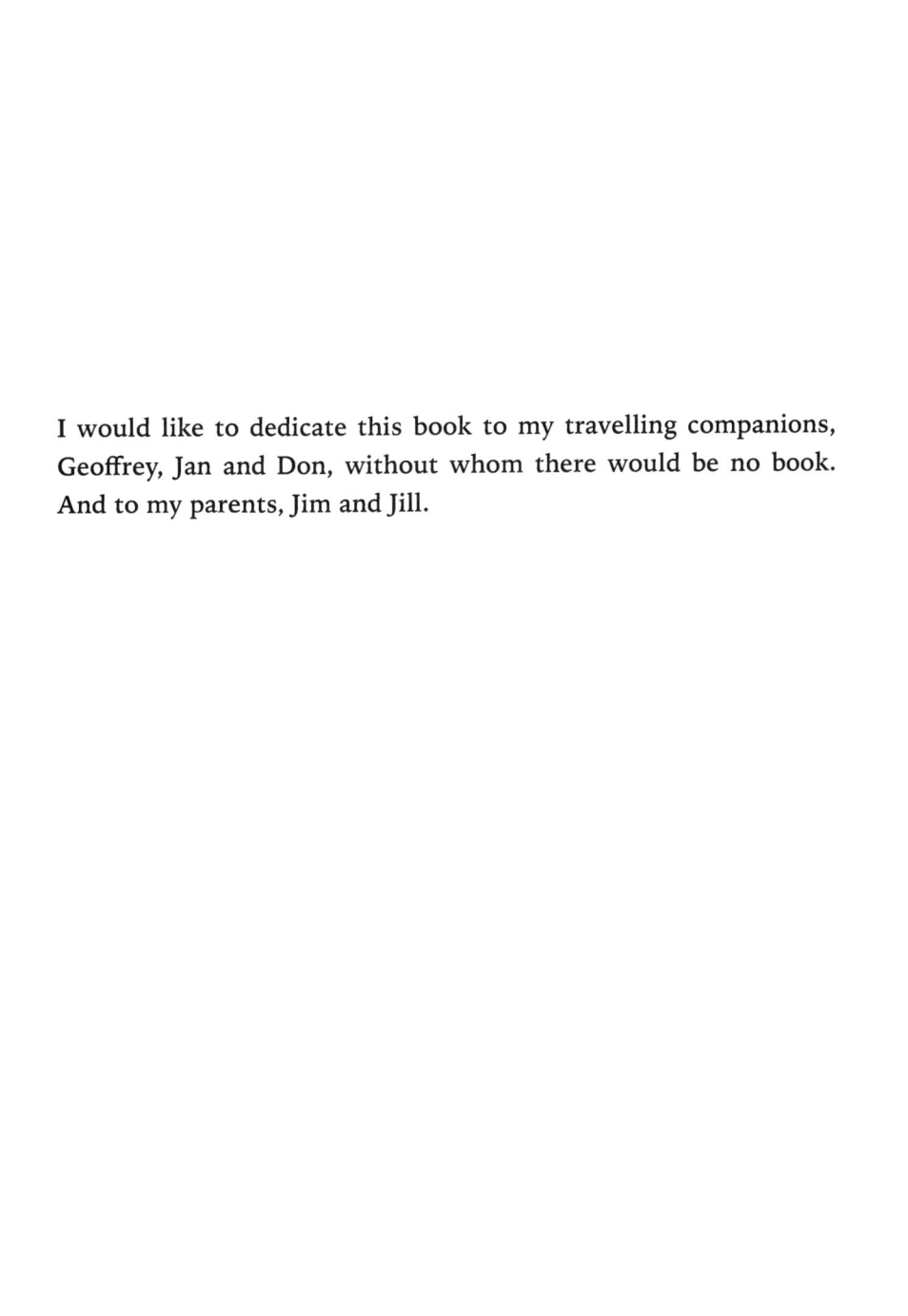

I would like to dedicate this book to my travelling companions, Geoffrey, Jan and Don, without whom there would be no book. And to my parents, Jim and Jill.

CONTENTS

Let Me Prepare You	1
1990 **Canada**	
Coyote Casserole	7
Boneshaker	11
2006 **Scotland, France and Italy**	
A Highland Fling	17
Blackbird Pie	25
Lake Como Epic	31
2012 **France and Italy**	
The Gypsy Horse Race	39
The Blood Bath	43
The Sausage Escapade	51
2014 **Greece, France, Italy, Croatia, Bosnia and Herzegovina, and the UAE**	
Patience, Madam. We're Taking You to the Special Needs Lounge	57
Not for the Unattractive	61
Lost in the Peloponnese	69
Gypsies and Fire	77
Pirate Island	81
Blind Ninjas Invade Collioure and What Not to Do at a Chic Mediterranean Beach	87
Couches and Coaches	97
La La Strikes Again and the Dangerous Creatures of Provence	103
We are NOT Going to Venice	109
Gypsies and Thieves	117
My Pelvic Floor Muscles Need Tightening	123

Give us a Fag, Sarge	129
How May We Not Help You?	135
How a Day at the Seaside Ends at a Prison for the Most Violent Mafioso in Italy	145
The Dagger	151

2018
Southeast Asia, Montenegro, Croatia, Italy and Oman

The Cruise from Hell	157
A Dose of Smallpox	167
Abruzzo Magic	173
Faulty Towers Tropea	181
Geoffrey Spits the Dummy and Sassy Goes into a Sulk	185
Driving over a Landslip	193
Goats and Gizzards	199
Hot Stuff	207
Message from the Author	215
Acknowledgements	217

LET ME PREPARE YOU

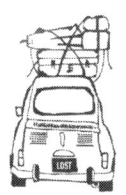

There are a few things you need to know before you read this book. This isn't an account of blissful family travels where we all have a lovely time then go home. Wrong book! But if you enjoy the realities of overseas adventures where everything that *can* go wrong does, punctuated with lots of laughs, crazy satnavs, domestics and a little bad language, then please join our crazy family for a rollickingly good time. We seem to have a talent for getting lost and attracting more than a normal amount of bad luck. To all our friends and family who have shared in our humorous tales of misfortune over the years and begged me to write a book—well here it is.

Travels with Geoffrey takes in the most hilarious and downright unbelievable travel adventures dating from pre-children in 1990 up until 2018 when my husband, Geoffrey, and I ventured off solo from New Zealand for the first time as empty nesters. So join us as we stumble our way through various episodes in Canada, Europe, Southeast Asia and Oman, flinging sausages and car parts, evading jails and facing the perils of typhoons, disease, abduction, wild coyotes, the Mafia and a car crash. All set to a backdrop of Geoffrey's entertaining outbursts and dubious driving.

Wherever I go, I write; pen and paper are always near. I love making people laugh so I hope that reading these anecdotes brings some enjoyment to your day and makes you smile.

Don't get me wrong; hard as it may be to believe after reading this book, there are an awful lot of days where things go *right*, but they don't make for fascinating reading, do they? What tend to stick in our minds long after the event are the disasters as they make the most entertaining memories.

We could take the easier option, travelling with guided holidays, cruises or bus tours, and given our track record, perhaps that would be wiser, but we choose to travel independently most of the time. Geoffrey's forced by our sizeable luggage collection, including gadgets and fans, to rent the largest and most un-Europe-friendly car possible. Just to explain the fans: I *do* fans. I have Singapore fan, man-fan (yes, really, a man-shaped fan), water-spraying fan and a biggish, swivel desk fan. As you may have guessed, I don't *do* heat. I also don't like deep water, boats or sharks or any combinations of the three. At my time of life, too much heat is likely to induce a hot flush, or it could be to do with the fact that I'm rather round.

Once the luggage collection is loaded, we then set off, full of hope for a blissful holiday. However, it all unravels pretty quickly and we spend most of our time lost and listening to Geoffrey having meltdowns. Just to forewarn you, Geoffrey's a pottymouth and when he gets frustrated he has the mental age of your average two-year-old having a tanty. I do apologise in advance for his occasional colourful language. I debated not including it but it's an integral part of the story and his character but I've tried to keep his rude words to a minimum and have bleeped some of them out. Don't get the wrong impression of Geoffrey though; he's usually a quiet, well-mannered, easy-going man who patiently gets led by his wife into some pretty sticky and stressful situations. He vents; we laugh.

I admittedly haven't helped by selecting properties to stay in locations that most sane people would never attempt to drive to. Luckily Geoffrey fancies himself as a bit of a pro driver, which is rather deluded of him given that he's had nine accidents. But he seems to revel in my driving challenges, tackling each situation like he's in a Formula One Grand Prix.

We stay in rental homes that meet my strict criteria, which means they must have air con, Wi-Fi, parking and a washing machine. Make of that what you will, although I've already explained about the heat and hot flushes, so you probably get the picture. A parking space is kind of mandatory when you cart around as much stuff as we do.

As the kids grew up, we learnt the hard way that Wi-Fi wasn't an option; it became a must. A couple of weeks in Sorrento on a trip with two teenagers and no Wi-Fi taught us an unforgettable lesson. Without Wi-Fi to entertain them, my darling children discovered the art of mimicry, copying every amusing phrase they heard American tourists utter, including their names. They had nothing against Americans but found their accents hilarious, much as Americans probably find ours disturbing. The kids assigned us all an American name, as overheard during their eavesdropping. Dad was Geoffrey. I became Denise and they were Jan and Don. Hence I'm using our allocated American names in this book. So in the absence of Wi-Fi, they honed their voices at night in our apartment, talking in a loud, American drawl until I thought Geoffrey was going to explode.

It got worse as the days wore on. Jan discovered she had a knack for doing a Borat voice and Don copied an Indian trying to sell us jewellery. Their talents knew no bounds, moving on to mimic the 'screaming goats' all the rage at the time on Facebook and YouTube. The goat sounds were the final straw for the poor family in the apartment above ours who one night started banging furiously on the floor with a broom. An hour later the landlord knocked on the door and said there had been a complaint regarding animals being kept in our apartment, possibly goats. He asked to have an inspection while the shameless Jan and Don stood grinning.

In response, the kids saved their voices for when we were on the road; everywhere we drove we were accompanied by Americans, goats, Borat and an Indian bead-seller. It became unbearable and Geoffrey finally blew, threatening to dump them at the side of the road in Naples and refuse to speak to them. We've never been without Wi-Fi or gadgets since. But the American names have stuck, to the point where my husband is only called Geoffrey; he doesn't even answer to his real name and the kids still insist on calling me Denise just to piss me off.

When we're not American tourists called Geoffrey and Denise, we work in the IT industry and as a kindergarten teacher respectively. I'm well known for being clumsy, having no coordination or balance and for attracting trouble wherever I go. I love to travel and when I'm not travelling I love to read about other people's travels and adventures. My favourite quote is 'The world is a book, and those who do not travel read only one page'. Travelling expands your view of the world and I love to see the differences and similarities between people, places and cultures and the alternative perspective it gives you on your own country.

Sadly we don't have the budget to match our desires and somewhat unwisely place travel as a priority ahead of a mortgage, cars, property maintenance and possessions. We may not be rich in monetary terms but we're rich in memories: memories of family adventures, the good, the bad, the ugly and the downright hilarious. We've given our children the gift of wanderlust and curiosity, the gift of tolerance and acceptance and of learning how to cope when things go wrong. They got plenty of practice at the latter.

1990

CANADA

COYOTE CASSEROLE

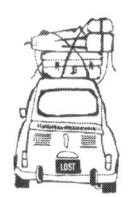

Geoffrey and I were touring Canada and Alaska in a campervan. As we'd explored Lake Louise and Banff, it was time to head north along the Icefields Parkway Highway towards Jasper. It had been a late spring; the thaw had yet to happen and the wildlife coming out of a long winter were extremely hungry and grouchy in their hunt for food. Everywhere we'd been, signs were warning of hungry bears hanging around. Their hunger makes them unpredictable and drives them closer to human habitat.

The late spring had caught us out, leaving us shivering through the nights in the bitterly cold conditions within our van. Waking each morning to ice crystals on the walls, we fought over whose turn it was to get up and boil water on the gas top to make hot coffee. We'd resorted to sleeping with all our clothes and jackets on and piling towels on top of the bedding for extra warmth. This wasn't a honeymoon van, that was for sure; any exposed skin would've grown icicles.

It was late when we set off north after spending the morning washing and drying our clothes at the local laundromat. Hence we found ourselves lacking a campground at the end of the day so stopped for the night at a pull-in area near Mount Murchison, aka the middle of nowhere in the Icefields Parkway National Park. No sign of life anywhere for miles, well not human anyway; animal was another story, as we were about to find out.

Geoffrey turned all alpha male and, with a Canadian beer in hand, tended to a campfire while I got all domesticated and put on a chicken and apricot casserole to cook. We wandered down to the nearby river while dinner was cooking. Probably not the wisest thing to do given that there were hungry bears around, we were in the middle of nowhere and there was now the delicious aroma of chicken wafting through the air. Suddenly we heard the sound of breaking vegetation and stopped, fully alert.

'Probably just a moose or deer,' said our alpha male Geoffrey.

Nevertheless we retraced our steps towards the campervan, trying not to break into a nervous run and look like sooky pants.[1] That was until we heard a distinct, growling sound.

'That's no moose,' I whispered. We cast pride aside and hightailed it to the van.

Alpha man downed another beer then stoked the fire, full of false bravado. I served the chicken and apricot casserole and brought it outside to dine al fresco in our camp chairs. What was I thinking? Our eating was disturbed by an ominously close-sounding growl. We looked up from our plates simultaneously.

'F#@%, f#@%, f#@%,' said Geoffrey in a tone of voice that clearly conveyed discomposure. Our eyes widened; our utensils hovered frozen in mid-air; we were staring directly into the eyes of a wild coyote. This was no Wile E. Coyote, cartoony-looking thing. Oh no. This one was a gnarly, half-starved, pissed-off one. Pissed off as in it had clearly been attacked by something else higher up the food chain. It was covered in blood, had one eye swollen shut and the way it was looking at us and our food said it wasn't prepared to come off second best this time.

'Shit! Run,' I shouted, simultaneously leaping to my feet and hurling my plate of chicken casserole towards the demented creature before sprinting for the safety of the van. Geoffrey followed in hot pursuit, also wisely choosing to toss his dinner at the coyote. The animal rushed forward, beginning a frenzied chow-down on our dinner, spitting out chunks of china, giving us time to slam the van door behind us.

'What shall we do?' I asked.

'Suppose we could have beans,' replied Geoffrey.

'I don't mean that! I mean should we stay here or move on?'

We both peered out of the window at Mr Coyote. Geoffrey decided we would just stay put and remain indoors as there wasn't any campsite nearby. We made some toast and sat down for a game of backgammon at the dining table. I glanced up.

'I don't believe it.' I groaned. The coyote, satiated and energised with casserole, was now stalking Bambi who just happened to be approaching our van on the other side, no doubt drawn by the smell of the food. Before I could yell out and warn Bambi, she was slaughtered next to our vehicle.

'Shit!' exclaimed Geoffrey. 'We're in the middle of the bloody killing fields.'

I whipped the curtains shut. I knew we were in the wilderness but this was a step too far. What next? If the food was drawing every starving animal in the area, there could be a bear next and a 200-kilo bear could smash its way through our flimsy van door. We heard a weird, huffing sound and peeped through the curtain. The coyote heard the same noise in the bush; its ears pricked up and it froze, mid-Bambi feast, lifted its nose and sniffed the air.

'It's a bear! It's a bear!' I shouted, hysteria rising. Geoffrey leapt into the driver's seat, gunned the engine and hightailed it out of there. We didn't stop driving for two hours. I sat reflecting on how many national park rules we'd broken: walking alone and unprotected in the wilderness, feeding the wildlife, littering with smashed crockery and leaving a fire unattended. How the hell were we going to survive Alaska? We needed to smarten up.

We reached Athabasca Falls at 11 p.m., where there was a picnic area to pull into. Thankfully there was one other campervan parked. Safety in numbers.

'I've gone right off chicken and apricot casserole,' I commented.

The next morning we went to sit outside to eat our cereal.

'Oh shit. We left the camp chairs behind,' muttered Geoffrey.

---

1. Cowardly.

BONESHAKER

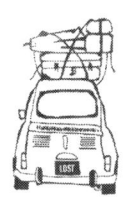

*G*eoffrey and I spent a month driving that campervan in a 4,786-kilometre loop between Vancouver, British Columbia, up through the Yukon and into Fairbanks, Alaska, before heading south again to Vancouver. Along the way we had a two-night break in between, courtesy of the Alaska Marine Highway ferry service, on board the MV *Taku*, which took us down the Inside Passage from Skagway to Prince Rupert.

We never planned on getting on a car ferry; we also never budgeted for it. In fact we couldn't afford it. 'Why were we on it?' you're probably wondering.

Well let's just say the Alaska Highway is a boneshaker and it doesn't just shake bones. It shakes crockery; it shakes cutlery; it shakes glassware; it shakes pots and pans; it shakes cupboards open; it shakes the fridge ajar; it shakes your eyeballs right out of your head. There's a reason they give out badges saying 'I survived the Alaska Highway' and it's nothing to do with the wildlife. If you can spend eight hours a day having the very life shaken out of you inside a tin can, you deserve that darned badge. The reason it's so rough is all the ruts caused by the constant freeze/thaw action on the road. No amount of road maintenance can keep up with Mother Nature. It's just the way it is.

Geoffrey and I crossed the border between British Columbia and the Yukon feeling excited that we would soon be crossing into Alaska. By the end of the next day, the mood on board had changed. The campervan started to shake; it began to shudder and the interior soon followed suit. Our first stop was for us to remove the cutlery drawers and stow them on the beds. A short while later, we stopped to secure the glassware, carefully wrapping it in tea towels and placing it on the bed alongside the cutlery drawers. Numerous stops later our bed looked like a white elephant sale; the cutlery and glassware had been joined by crockery, pots, pans, bottles and pantry items. Socks were now useful vessels for bottles.

Our heads pounded. The wardrobe door began swinging open, periodically disgorging its contents over the floor. The fridge was feeling left out so joined the wardrobe door in a merry dance which the bathroom door felt it should be included in too. Our bathroom contents landed on the floor, including in the toilet. The sound inside the R.V was deafening. Even tape cassettes by Roxette and Phil Collins couldn't drown out the cacophony; they just added to the overall din. We stopped by the roadside and got out. We would have sat on our camp chairs, only they were gone. I pictured the coyote sitting back chilling on one of the chairs by the fire, patiently awaiting the next chicken casserole. We plonked ourselves on the ground and looked around, savouring the peace and quiet and resting our bone-shaken bodies.

It was time to make a plan as there were three more days of bone-jarring racket until we made Fairbanks, and what goes up north needs to come back down south. Hence we took the decision to splurge on a car ferry from Skagway to Prince Rupert on our return journey. This would give our jiggering heads a reprieve from driving. Could we afford it? No. Could we face the full return journey of this bone-shaking symphony? No. Decision made. Coming back we would get the ferry if they had space for us and the campervan.

They did, but there were no cabins. Once on board I quickly

assessed our comfort options: food—dodgy cafeteria selling stale items; sleep—deckchairs in the open air that were at least flat if you didn't mind the sub-arctic temperatures and howling wind, or hard chairs in the lounge that didn't recline; bathroom facilities—ladies or gents communal showers with a row of showerheads and no separation for privacy, or option B—stink. The tiled wet room looked as if it was straight out of a penitentiary facility with the added thrill of being ventilated by a row of open-air windows above the showerheads opening to the Gulf of Alaska. This at least ensured a quick turnaround under the faucets before hypothermia set in.

What a night that first one was. We were trying hard to get to sleep on lounge chairs when dozens of school children on a trip got on board at Haines. Once their excitement died down, we were still left trying to sleep in a room full of people coming and going, whispering, snoring and grunting like pigs. We were unsurprisingly still awake and very grumpy when the ship docked at Juneau at 2 a.m. amidst much clanking, clanging and engine noise, so Geoffrey ducked down to the campervan and returned with all our pillows, blankets and sleeping bags. We set up beds on the hard floor in the forward lounge and finally got a couple of hours' sleep. I was woken at 4:30 a.m. by the ship rocking as we passed through a bit of a storm. Peeping out of the window in the early morning light, I could make out a few icebergs. *Oh no. That's all we need, picturing the Titanic!*

As I looked around me, I was surprised to see everyone else had copied us and we were now surrounded by a sea of camping bodies strewn around the floor with no one using the uncomfortable seats. I decided to tiptoe off to the open-air shower while everyone was still asleep. No way was I showering in front of complete strangers. On my way back to my sleeping bag, I carefully surveyed the waters lest I needed to alert the captain of any icebergs that I considered a threat. Thankfully they were tiddlers and I went back to sleep for a few hours. A hearty American breakfast set us up for a day of pacing, reading, yawning and wildlife spotting. Score: one group of dolphins, three sea otters and my sunglasses which were whipped right off my head and joined the sea life.

Just as we and our fellow cabinless travellers were bedding down for another night on the floor and in various stages of undress, the front row cried out, 'WHALES!' I've never seen such a rush in my life. I staggered out of my sleeping bag and ran barefooted to the window, screaming, 'Geoffrey, grab the camera!' I reached the window in time to see four orca whales breach above the water in an almighty synchronised leap. I raced for the deck, assembling along the handrail outside beside my fellow pyjama-clad inmates. The orcas were by now specks on the horizon.

I wriggled my frozen toes then looked around and laughed out loud. How absurd we looked: hair astray, flying in the wind; ladies with night cream dabbed on faces; nightwear in clashing styles and colours; super-hero pyjamas. It was no wonder the whales had altered course. The ship was starting to rock a bit and we were all wide awake, wired on adrenaline.

When we stopped briefly at Ketchikan, Geoffrey and I hopped off for a quick leg stretch then settled down to sleep on the floor at 10:30 p.m. We slept well until 4 a.m. when a horrendous, crackling din echoed around the lounge from the speakers. The announcement amounted to, 'Get up! We dock in 45 minutes.' Despicable despots.

2006

SCOTLAND, FRANCE AND ITALY

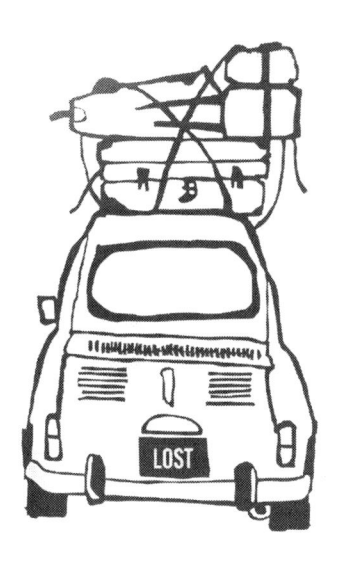

A HIGHLAND FLING

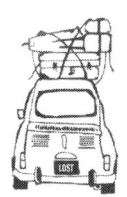

*L*iving in New Zealand means that Europe's a long way and the travel costs so much money that to make the expense worthwhile, it makes sense to go for as long as you can. Geoffrey and I had scrimped and saved to take Jan and Don, thirteen and six respectively, on an eleven-week trip around Europe. Our children's school principal gave us his blessing and their teachers gave them some printed sheets for them to work on reading, writing and maths then told them to keep a diary and asked Jan to complete a project. The principal's opinion was that our children would learn far more from seeing the world than anything they would learn in school. He was right; they saw Greek and Roman history, discovered so much about different countries and their geography, and picked up a smattering of French and Italian.

Three weeks into the trip, and with Disneyland California, Cornwall and the Lake District under our belts, we'd now arrived in Scotland. Travel so far had involved two children in the back seat periodically doing homework on their fold-down trays, talking, laughing, listening to music, snoozing or watching the scenery go by while asking questions about where we were going or what they'd just seen.

The day dawned sunny and warm in Plockton on the west coast of the Scottish Highlands. It's better known to most people as the small fishing village used as the setting for the television series *Hamish Macbeth*. It was this that drew us there and we weren't disappointed; our week in this quaint and authentic, whitewashed village had been a pleasure. We'd stayed as guests of the local hotel on the waterfront, the waterside garden bar providing a perfect spot for watching the Zodiacs zipping ashore with passengers from boats moored in the bay. Each evening my eyes were drawn to the supposedly abandoned castle across the water; it looked so mysterious in the moonlight and I could've sworn I saw flickering candlelight from within.

It wasn't only *Hamish Macbeth* that had lured me there; it was also the book *Ring of Bright Water* by Gavin Maxwell which was set near Plockton and had sent us off on a search for the bay where Gavin had lived with the otters. We found what we thought was the entrance to the long drive down to the bay from the road above but NO ACCESS signs blocked it off. We visited the general area though and a little local museum where Don bought a soft-toy otter.

He'd spent the week living on dinosaur Twizzlers[1] and doing school work in a lively bar while we enjoyed a ceilidh or two. He could barely write but kept a daily journal that talked non-stop about daggers, swords and snakes. In later years one particular dagger would almost land us in jail in Dubai, but more of that later. His snake obsession was thanks to Skye Serpentarium Reptile Refuge, a rescue centre on the Isle of Skye. His enthusiasm had forced us to visit it twice; it was a major novelty factor for him as New Zealand is entirely without serpents.

Jan on the other hand had enjoyed fine dining, including a brief foray into the Scottish tradition of haddock with scrambled egg; it was a one-off experience. She put up with doing maths in the bar and had loved the castles, history and travelling. But now it was time to finish packing and load the car. We were off for a week exploring the Northern Highlands with no plans or booked accommodation. Ah, such freedom.

As we finished loading our luggage into the car boot on the

waterfront, the landlady came running out to us and insisted we take with us their only copy of the *Scottish Accommodation Guide* as she was concerned we didn't have anywhere booked. Unbeknown to us it was a long weekend. Not only that but the last long weekend before winter. We said our farewells with a sense of foreboding. For those who don't know me, I'm super organised; I never leave things to chance and always book in advance. But our good friends had said I should try just winging it. 'Enjoy the freedom of stopping at will for the night when you feel like it,' said they. Sounded great in theory.

With the boot now stacked to the ceiling, we hopped in and Geoffrey reversed. There was a terrible crunching sound and smashing glass. We all looked at each other and sighed. *Geoffrey strikes again*, I thought. Geoffrey had form. He'd already reversed into a stone wall in Mousehole, Cornwall, just three weeks prior.

Oh, the humiliation. It was made worse by a crowd gathering and some bearded old chap yelling, 'Stop! Don't leave the scene!' as he held his hand out in the universal stop signal, standing in front of our bonnet like we were about to zoom off and disappear. His voice rose in hysteria as Geoffrey ignored him and moved the car. He was just getting it off the street but the frenzied loon was convinced we were absconding and sent someone running into a nearby shop to fetch the owner of the car we'd hit. Jan and I slunk down in our seats. Don watched with interest, waving his small dagger in one hand and a toy rubber snake in the other. Geoffrey muttered something about Scottish tossers.

He bravely hopped out to face the wrath of the locals and deal with the owner of the vehicle who'd just arrived. All of Plockton watched. Where was Hamish Macbeth when you needed him? Luckily for us the owner was a good-natured fellow who took it all in his stride. Damage was minimal so we exchanged insurance details and we were ready to resume departure.

'That must be our bad luck out of the way for the day,' I announced with false bravado.

We headed into the wilds of the Highlands and relaxed. The scenery was spectacular, all towering granite peaks, boulders, golden grasses and heathers interspersed with lochs. In the middle of a valley floor, we stopped to inspect an abandoned stone croft. This involved leaping across a small stream and walking through sinking peat moss with our feet disappearing beneath the turf. I was terrified I would step into a legendary Scottish bog, never to be seen again. We examined the ancient and crumbling croft with interest. Don waved his little dagger about in a frenzy, warding off giant mozzies,[2] before we scuttled back to the car.

Geoffrey spotted an awesome photo opportunity and suddenly swerved at high speed into a pull-in area. The car was thrown into a deep pothole with the second ominous crunch of the day, this time from underneath the vehicle. A domestic followed in which I accused Geoffrey of damaging the car again; a fact which he strongly refuted.

Twenty kilometres later, in the middle of a rocky mountain pass, we heard the sound of something under the car scraping the road. *Gee, now there's a surprise*, I thought, folding my arms and casting an accusing glare in Geoffrey's direction. He pulled over and got out to investigate. I hopped out and came around one side of the car in time to see Geoffrey throwing a large, black piece of metal into the heather.

'What's that?' I asked.

'Oh, just some part of the undercarriage but don't worry, we won't be needing it,' came the reply.

'Are you actually insane? Geoffrey, it's part of the car. Won't they require it back when we return the vehicle?'

No response.

We stopped at Gairloch, a little coastal village, to look for food and wandered into an art and jewellery shop. I was immediately attracted to a stunning painting of a kingfisher; it was huge but I just had to have it. I got talking to the owner who had a connection to New Zealand as she and her husband had a second home in Omarama where her husband glided, fished and painted. He'd painted the kingfisher there, which he took back to Scotland and which was now going back to New Zealand with me.

The owner asked if we'd ever watched *Hamish Macbeth* and on learning we loved it and had just come from Plockton, she proceeded to entertain us with true-life stories about their very own village policeman. They went as follows…

Story number one
A gentleman crashed his car into their fence one night and was hanging over it. She peered through the window then rang the village policeman.
'But, Marie, I'm in bed. Does he look drunk?' he asked.
'I don't know,' she said.
'Well go and ask him then ask him if he's on drugs,' said the local bobby.[3]

Story number two
The post office alarm went off in the night and Marie rang the bobby.
'I'm in bed. Is there anyone dangerous in the post office?' he asked.
'I don't know,' she retorted.
'Well can you go and look?' suggested our wonderful policeman.

Story number three
There was a wedding outside the village with everyone in attendance and well inebriated. They had a new and overly keen village bobby. He stationed himself at the gate, waiting to catch drunk villagers leaving the wedding.
'What did you do?' we asked Marie.
'Well,' she said, 'we had a whip-round and raised £40 which we gave to the village boy racer when we were all ready to leave. He zoomed out of the gate at high speed and the policeman followed him. Meanwhile the villagers were all able to drive home.'
They then rang a farmer a few miles out of town and told him the policeman was coming and could he arrange a welcome reception. After the boy racer went past, the farmer released his sheep onto the road and the bobby crashed the police car. He was later transferred to Inverness.

Story number four
Another overly enthusiastic bobby managed to annoy all the local fishermen so they stole his car and transferred it by boat to a little offshore island where it sat, lights and siren flashing, until its battery died. He got the message and asked for a transfer.

After we'd enjoyed all the local tales and scandals, we left Gairloch behind and carried on to Ullapool, that night's planned destination, as it was the only sizeable town within hundreds of miles. But we drove into bedlam; there was a huge music festival on in town, with tents and marquees set up in fields, police everywhere and inebriated revellers staggering all over the road. We paused as a group of men dressed as nurses danced around our car to loud cheers from passersby. Don's eyes were out on stalks as he waved his toy snake at them. Every motel and hotel had NO VACANCY signs up. We were forced to carry on out the other side of town, stressed about where on earth we would find to stay overnight given that there were no towns on the map for many miles.

Our friends' comments rang in my ears. 'Just wing it,' they'd said. 'For once in your life, don't be so organised.' Yeah well, look where that had got us. *Never again!* I thought, only to forget in future.

A few minutes later, we came over the crest of a hill and down towards a beautiful, sweeping bay. On our right was a group of three whitewashed crofters cottages with a B&B sign on one of them saying the magical word—VACANCY.

We couldn't believe our luck and pulled in, hoping it was true and not just that they hadn't changed their sign over. A lovely lady came out to greet us and said she'd just that minute swapped it over as she'd had a last-minute cancellation; divine intervention perhaps. The room was just a double but she was concerned that we wouldn't find anywhere to stay so insisted that it was no trouble for her to add a futon bed and a mattress to the room for Don and Jan.

She introduced herself as Lucy and showed us the room, which was lovely, with beautiful views of the bay and the Summer Isles beyond. It had its own little dining room, outdoor table, swing seat and garden. Don headed outside to leap from rock to rock, brandishing his toy sword, while we got sorted. Lucy's son carried down a futon and mattress which she set up with bedding. It was a snug fit but we had every home comfort made all the more comforting by Lucy's care for a family in need. She brought the children chocolate and got us afternoon tea and iced lemon water.

That night we retired to our cosy oasis after a long day. I was lying on the bed looking at all the books on the shelf when it hit me. I sat up like a bolt.

'She's Lucy Irvine,' I gasped.

'Who?' asked Geoffrey.

'You know, the author of *Castaway* and *Faraway*. Look! Her books are here on the shelf. I've read all of them.'

And sure enough, there was her photo on the inside cover, definitely her. By coincidence, on the shelf was another book I love called *A Last Wild Place* by Mike Tomkies about his time in the wilds of Western Scotland. Well I never, what a day of surprises.

We had a lovely breakfast with Lucy who'd been out and picked us some wild brambles and blackberries to go with our porridge and prepared a cooked breakfast as well. She gave Jan and me signed notes for our journals and asked us to send more lovely New Zealanders her way. I spoke to her about her time on the Pacific Islands while Don bounded off outside again to leap from one giant glacial rock to another and Lucy sat entranced. She said Don was gorgeous; watching him took her back in time to when her boys were young and would do the same thing.

With heartfelt thanks and goodbyes, we reluctantly dragged ourselves away from Ardmair, refreshed after meeting this amazing woman. When I returned to New Zealand, I got her books out of the library and re-read them all. I follow her on Facebook and she now lives in Bulgaria where she's set up a charity to rescue, feed and reduce the suffering of abandoned or stray dogs, cats and horses in this poverty-stricken country.

---

1. Dinosaur-shaped chicken nuggets.
2. Mosquitoes.
3. Slang for policeman.

BLACKBIRD PIE

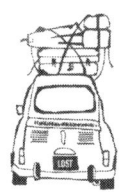

I awoke wondering briefly where I was, disorientated after weeks on the road. Jan was so befuddled by sleeping in different rooms every night that she'd been stumbling around sleepwalking, trying to leave via any exit she could find. One night I found her about to depart Fitzgerald's Hotel at 3 in the morning.

I sat bolt upright. *Shit. I've remembered where I am. I'm in Tramore, Ireland, and the alarm should've gone off at 5:30 a.m. Shit, shit, shit.* It was 6:30 and we had a ferry to catch from Rosslare to Fishguard in Wales. I leapt from the bed, screeching like a demented banshee at everyone to get up. We all ran in circles, flinging things in bags; well, everyone except Don who was still lying in bed looking dazed.

He sleepily climbed into some clothes I gave him and Jan helped by flinging his stuff in his bag. We tiptoed out of the B&B, rather pointlessly after all the screaming and banging. After a tense drive to the ferry terminal in Rosslare, we whistled onto the port just in time to be waved straight on board. The ferry departed on time at 9 for the three-hour crossing. Settling in, Geoffrey snoozed (which turned out to be a wise move) while Jan and Don worked on their maths and Don caught up on his journal to take back to school after our trip.

We disembarked the ferry just after 12:30 and found our way

onto the M4 motorway with a plan to stop for the night a bit later at one of the large motorway services. These are massive places with petrol station, hotel, restaurants, shops, toilets and showers. About 5 p.m., we reached the Outer London ring road and traffic came to a standstill. The kids had had enough and Jan led Don in a rendition of the song '99 Bottles of Beer'. All we could hear were their sing-song voices chanting '99 bottles of beer on the wall, 99 bottles of beer. Take one down and pass it around, 98 bottles of beer on the wall' and on and on it went. Don thought it was great and waved Gary, his soft-toy crocodile, in time to the tune while Geoffrey quietly lost the will to live. As soon as we were through the London traffic, we were eager to stop for the night; we were tired and hungry. Plus by now we were up to about 47 bottles of beer on the wall. *Enough's enough, Jan!* It was a simple plan. What could go wrong? The problem we hadn't anticipated was that it was Wednesday.

At the following motorway services, we pulled in and went into the hotel to book a room. Unfortunately it was fully booked. The receptionist informed us that Wednesday nights were always booked out by businessmen and work travellers. She tried a few places in the local town for us but all were full so she rang ahead to the next services and the next. It was the same everywhere: not on a Wednesday, sorry. This problem hadn't even occurred to us. What had I said in Scotland about never again winging it? It was now dark and the kids were hungry so we ate dinner in silence before being forced to continue.

On we drove, across almost the entire width of the UK. Yes, you read that right. Not only that but we'd started the day in Ireland. In the rear-view mirror, I could see the kids nodding off, Don asleep in his car seat, clutching Gary the crocodile, probably dreaming about the incompetence of his parents who had somehow missed the memo entitled 'Not on a Wednesday'.

Finally at 9 p.m., only 21 miles from Dover, we found a very posh hotel in Ashford where the business fraternity on a mid-week conference had kindly left the family suite free.

'This will be the most expensive few hours we've ever spent sleeping,' muttered Geoffrey.

Jan and Don quickly settled into bed, asleep in an instant. I on the other hand was awake for hours, leaping about with cramp from being in a car for hours. I prayed the next day would go a bit more to plan.

We slept in, enjoying a leisurely breakfast before heading off to Dover about 10 a.m. We were waved onto an earlier ferry bound for Calais, leaving us with time on our side to find our B&B in the Champagne region en route to Provence.

Naturally the time we'd gained was lost by a monumental cockup on the French autoroute. Needless to say it was all my fault and caused a major domestic. Geoffrey was overjoyed to have to pay the French autoroute toll twice to cover the same section of road for 60 kilometres in both directions. He was in a right tizzy.

I ignored Geoffrey's negative vibes and admired the passing countryside, historic abbeys, rolling pasture and vineyards as well as glimpses of pretty villages. There was a conversation going on in the back seat that I didn't quite catch but I heard Jan saying something about blackbirds.

Regardless of my questionable navigational skills in French, we somehow managed to locate the rural B&B on a large working farm where we were staying overnight. As we pulled into the courtyard, we noticed the massive stables and farm buildings to one side while the farmhouse in front of us was an impressive, three-storey, slightly jaded-looking stone structure.

As Geoffrey insisted that he didn't trust the French and was there under sufferance (he hadn't got over the bombing of the *Rainbow Warrior*[1]), I'd been placed in charge of learning some travel French. I was apprehensive but the farmer's wife had assured me via email that she spoke reasonable English and would be there for our arrival. Geoffrey shoved me forward and I nervously pulled on the giant-sized door knocker. The door slowly creaked open and before us stood a stereotypical caricature of a French farmer. We gaped. He fired off a whole volley of rapid French while his moustache twitched. Only *bonjour* sounded vaguely familiar. I timidly asked in French if he spoke

English. '*Non*,' was the firm reply. Oh shit. I resorted to paper and whipped out our booking while enquiring after *madame*'s absence. She'd been called away.

Our French farmer showed us up to our two rooms which were on the third floor. Geoffrey muttered darkly to himself as he carted the luggage up three flights of creaking wooden stairs. The rest of us were in absolute awe of the house, the size of it and how old it must be. New Zealand, a relatively young country, has very few historic buildings. Here everything creaked: the stairs, the beds and the plumbing. The bathroom on the landing outside our rooms made horrendous, rumbling plumbing noises when we used the toilet or sink. The rooms were decorated in what appeared to be genuine and original furnishings with tapestries, heavy curtains and wrought-iron beds. So French. I was very excited.

'It's old, dusty, peeling and tatty,' muttered Geoffrey.

'It's probably haunted,' Jan told Don.

The farmer called us downstairs, showing us into a massive drawing room where he gave us all a champagne apéritif, including little Don. The room was filled with the most amazing 16th-century carved Henry III furniture but what impressed us most were the enormous, grand tapestries and paintings on the wall that easily spanned three metres, depicting religious, hunting and farming scenes. The farmer did his best to speak to us with a few stilted words of English conveying that his wife was in Paris shopping and had left him in charge. The housekeeper had dinner all prepared and would be in to serve us breakfast in the morning as he would be working on the farm. His children were in the next room where there was a television playing *Harry Potter* in French. Three charming, eight-week-old kittens gambolled around the place, playfully attacking each other.

The farmer called us through to the dining room, a room even more impressive than the last, where he did a fine job of serving us. First he offered us a drink, refusing with horror our request for white wine, for no, we were having beef; he couldn't condone allowing white wine with beef. What were we, peasants? He went off to get the red wine and some juice for the kids. I noticed Don looked like he was going to cry and asked what was wrong.

'Jan told me they eat blackbird pies in France. I don't want to eat a blackbird,' he stammered.

Oh, so that's what the blackbird conversation in the car was about, I thought. 'Well it's true they eat birds,' I said, 'but don't worry. I don't think we're having any sort of pie.'

So imagine, if you will, Don's face when the farmer returned with a silver tray and presented us each with a little pastry pie, about the right size to contain one blackbird within. When he left the room, Jan couldn't wait to say, 'See, Don, it's a blackbird pie,' and began reciting the nursery rhyme 'Four and Twenty Blackbirds'. I thought Don would burst into tears so I quickly inspected the pie and found it was beef and mushroom. Crisis averted and Jan was kicked under the table.

Our first-ever posh French dinner was interrupted by screams of terror as Don leapt onto his chair, clutching his legs. One of the kittens had found its way into the grand dining room and was launching surprise attacks with its claws on his legs, not to mention trying to climb the tablecloth. The noise alerted the farmer to the kitten's presence and he shooed it out before presenting us with a beautiful beef and tomato casserole, beans and bread followed by an apple tart for dessert. Geoffrey was starting to thaw in his attitude towards the French. Perhaps they weren't so bad after all. Completely full we made our way upstairs. The kittens spotted our exit, scampering behind. Don ran ahead up the three flights of stairs, screaming in terror.

Everyone got ready for bed and Don kept a wary eye out for ghosts. The house creaked; the lumpy mattress sagged; the bed groaned and Geoffrey snored. That was until I went to the loo. The whole place suddenly reverberated with clanging pipes.

---

1. A bombing operation by the French in 1985 to sink Greenpeace's *Rainbow Warrior* in the Port of Auckland, New Zealand.

LAKE COMO EPIC

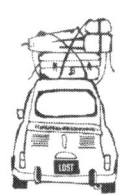

*S*everal nights later, after a glorious week in Provence, Geoffrey and I lay awake, not wanting our time in France to be over. He'd come to France under protest but Provence had woven its magic on him and he was now a firm Francophile, eager to return. I got up, leaning out of the shutters to gaze down at the village square below, soaking it all in: the flitting bats dancing around in the street light, the warm evening air filled with the chirping of cicadas, occasionally interrupted by melodic church bells chiming.

The romantic image of French life that we'd read about in Peter Mayle's books certainly did exist in rural Provence in the Luberon Valley. Geoffrey's preconceived notion that all French people would be arrogant tossers proved unfounded. In fact the opposite was true; they'd been an absolute delight, patiently and with much good humour attempting to help us through our French linguistic nightmares.

The village baker appeared to thoroughly enjoy our morning ritual where we pretended to order our baguettes and lemon tarts in French while he allowed our language faux pas charades to continue for the amusement of all in the shop. A big grin would spread across his creased and dusty face just at the sight of us entering.

The next day dawned and we reluctantly set off early, knowing that we had a long drive ahead to get to Lake Como in Italy. We stuck to the autoroute, heading directly south from Provence to the Mediterranean coast where we turned to head east along the French Riviera high above Cannes, Nice and Monaco. Surprisingly, for hundreds of kilometres we were nowhere near the ground. The entire autoroute following the coastline consisted of vertiginous, repeating, high-rise viaducts towering in mid-air, strung between mountain tunnels. I read later that there were exactly one hundred tunnels on this stretch of autoroute and the same number of harrowingly narrow viaducts. To add to the danger, the road was all sweeping curves and the main route for large articulated trucks going at 130 kilometres per hour. It was terrifying.

At the first Italian *autostrada* (Italian motorway) stop after crossing the border, we were bewildered with culture shock and the noise created by dozens of Italians all talking and gesticulating at once. Oh the chaos; it was amazing. There was absolutely no concept of forming a queue for food or coffee. They had a bizarre system set up for ordering, which we later realised maximised the opportunity for personal contact and talking. It was sheer craziness but there was no point in fighting it; it was simply how they did things there. When in Rome, as they say.

The lady with the ultimate power over the caffeine refused to serve one poor hapless guy as she didn't like his attitude; she told him to go away, even though he'd paid for his coffee and was frantically waving his receipt at her. She stood her ground and he was forced to move on in search of caffeine elsewhere. France was so orderly and polite but this wasn't. Even the road on the French side was orderly, whereas the Italian side remained defiantly indifferent to order.

We sat with our well-earned coffee and food and watched with interest. What stood out were the Italian men: tall, dark and handsome, all using any reflective surface at all to preen, smoothing hair, adjusting expensive sunglasses or patting down shirts and belts. You could smell the aroma of leather and good grooming.

Feeling self-conscious we dragged ourselves away from the overt display of pure style, trying our best to smarten ourselves up. Back on the road we found ourselves running very late. By the time we got to the town of Como, it was already dark, not ideal conditions for locating a holiday rental.

Not surprisingly we took a wrong turn. There was no satnav or Google maps; this was the days of paper maps. It was too dark to see my map and the signs were now all in Italian. It had been my job on this trip to learn some French, which I'd studied fastidiously, leaving Geoffrey to learn Italian. He assured us he was completely au fait with the language after months with the phrase book and CDs. However, it became apparent soon after crossing the border into Italy that Geoffrey's knowledge of Italian amounted to being able to say pizza, spaghetti, espresso, gelato and *buon giorno* (good morning). His pièce de résistance was to tack an 'o' onto the end of every word and wave his arms around wildly like an Italian.

There were some particularly important-looking road signs illuminated ahead. I optimistically asked Geoffrey what they meant. Not a clue! This could be one monumental problem but to be fair I hadn't exactly shone at French navigation.

We came to a halt in a queue of traffic. As we crawled forward, we were surrounded by further large and significant-looking signs clearly trying to tell us something important. I again asked Geoffrey the official Italian interpreter what they said but as they weren't announcing pizza or gelato, he remained oblivious. My anxiety levels rose. As we inched closer in the darkness, we suddenly saw Swiss flags followed by signs showing passports. With dawning horror we realised we were at the Swiss border and about to enter Switzerland.

'Shit,' shouted Geoffrey, who reacted swiftly just before the point of no return, doing a sharp turn and trying desperately to escape the border crossing. 'How the hell did we nearly end up in Switzerland?' he asked with some exasperation.

'I'd quite like to go to Switzerland,' commented Jan from the back seat. 'They make good chocolate.'

It was now very late, dark and starting to rain. The mood in the car was tense, with everyone tired and on edge as we retraced our route to the missing Lake Como.

'We were at the town of Como. The lake's only the third-largest in all of Italy so how the hell did we end up in Switzerland?' muttered Geoffrey.

With the elusive lake finally now in sight, we set off along its edge for many, many miles, searching for the turnoff to the village where our rental house was located. The road was narrow and sinewy, twisting between tall stone buildings rising straight up from the road edge inches from our car.

After an exceedingly long and strained journey, we located our exit with a sense of relief and horror. Horror as the exit would appear to take us vertically up the side of a flipping great mountain. Four pairs of eyes strained upwards; five if you counted Gary. Geoffrey groaned. I sighed. Even the car protested as it struggled in first gear on the steep slope. There was dead silence in the car after that; I think we were too scared to speak. The torturous, switchback road tapered to a single lane barely wide enough for one vehicle. On one side was a plunging drop back down to the lake's edge far below in the darkness.

On and on, up and up we went, leaving all the lights far below us. The only sound was the roar of the straining engine. Just before we reached the blackness of the chestnut forests on the ridgetop, we came across a house with all the lights on and an open gate; we were there.

'Thank God.' I sighed with relief.

'They could be axe murderers,' muttered Jan helpfully.

'Shut up,' said Geoffrey.

'No one would hear us scream up here,' she added.

'For God's sake,' snapped Geoffrey.

Gary meowwwed. Yes, Don's soft-toy crocodile meows; it's a long story.

The owner's house was just below ours and as they'd seen the approaching headlights, they came to greet us and let us in. It was a beautiful, modern, A-line mountain chalet and had it not been for the need to buy food, we would have remained put for the week, too terrified to face the road down. Once the kids were sorted, fed and in bed, we collapsed, trying to blot out all thoughts of the day's drive.

I awoke next morning, struggling to remember where I was, then opened the bedroom shutters, flooding the room with light. I couldn't believe what I saw and woke Geoffrey to come and look. We were so high up, we were eye to eye with a glacier. The sky was blue and the glory of Lake Como and all the villages stretched out far below us. Just then the Sunday morning church bells from the village beneath echoed around the valley. It was stunning. But getting back down that mountain to get food was going to take some courage after last night. We couldn't imagine what would happen if we met a car coming the opposite way.

Just then Don came running upstairs. 'I saw a salamander,' he announced proudly.

We just looked at him. 'How do you even know what a salamander is?' I asked. 'You're six years old. And more importantly, just where have you been to see a salamander?'

'Don't worry. I didn't touch it. I know they're poisonous.'

'Shit,' said Geoffrey, his standard response to most situations.

'Where's Jan?' I asked.

'Oh, she's watching "SpongeBob SquarePants" on TV. It's in German.'

2012

FRANCE AND ITALY

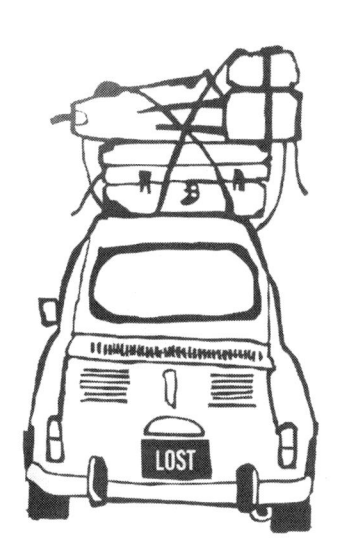

THE GYPSY HORSE RACE

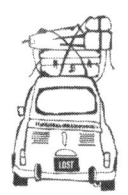

We'd left New Zealand on our travels again as our first family trip to Europe had resulted in a constant yearning to return there. So after six years of saving every penny, here we were. Jan had just turned nineteen and Don was twelve. After an early start following a layover in Dubai, we flew to Nice in the South of France, landing just after lunch to a stunning 32°C day. Geoffrey rang the Eurolease car office and they sent a man to meet us who transferred us over to their depot near the terminal. He introduced us to our brand-spanking-new vehicle and after a five-minute introductory talk, left Geoffrey with the keys. I don't know who was more nervous—Geoffrey or the rest of us.

The four of us climbed aboard, ready to begin our next adventures abroad. But first we needed to guide our unfamiliar new wheels safely out of Nice Airport on the opposite side of the road to what we were used to. We turned on the satnav, who we christened Marjorie thanks to her very commanding voice, and headed onto the first roundabout. *No more maps! Hooray, gone are the days of getting lost*, I thought. Twenty-five minutes later, after doing numerous laps of the airport and the same roundabouts and with much hilarity from the back-seat drivers, we finally left. From there we headed west towards Aix-en-Provence to find somewhere to stay. We didn't plan on driving far given fatigue was a factor after travelling for 48 hours already from New Zealand.

When we'd looked at accommodation online, the hotels in and around Nice were all too expensive so the plan was to head to the next biggish town and find a hotel well away from all the glitz and glamour of Nice and the associated glitzy prices. The weather was glorious and the scenery beautiful; all was right with the world. We were filled with that carefree feeling you get at the start of a holiday. At the first autoroute road services, we stopped for petrol, food, coffee, wine and souvenirs. What a treasure trove it was. We were on a bit of a high and our basket overflowed with every sort of tacky souvenir known to mankind containing or depicting lavender, lemons or cicadas. It was our first rusty foray into tentatively testing our limited tourist French in six years, interspersed with much laughter, miming and raised eyebrows. And still the sun shone and that quintessential Provençal light lulled us into a sense of bliss.

We approached the autoroute toll booths with a sense of blind panic at all the unfamiliar signs in French and foolishly got into the credit-card lane, with a line of honking French behind us; there was no escape. Our New Zealand credit cards didn't work in the machine so we had to press the help button and wait for rescue, much to the fury of all those stuck impatiently at our rear. Oh, the humiliation. Once rescued by the attendant, we made our way to Aix-en-Provence but foolishly decided to keep going as it was easy driving on the autoroute and we were soaking up the stunning Provençal views. According to the map, Arles was coming up, where Vincent Van Gogh had lived and painted for a period of time, so we decided to stop there for the night.

My visions of sunflowers and starry skies were quickly vanquished. Arles didn't appear to want us. As we tried to enter, we were faced with a detour and barricades. There were cars and strangely dressed people everywhere but we didn't understand any of the French signs. To add to our confusion, the crowd appeared to be all gypsies, but why and what was going on?

For reasons known only to himself, or perhaps due to fatigue, Geoffrey got fed up with getting the run-around trying to enter Arles.

He bypassed a set of barriers, driving through a throng of gypsies who were wandering all over the road. They seemed to be shouting something at us.

'I don't think we're meant to be here, Dad,' yelled Jan.

Once we were through the blockade of people, it became immediately obvious why the road was blocked off as a bunch of horses adorned with gypsies thundered past uncomfortably close to our car. Don's and Jan's eyes bulged.

'Shit,' shouted Geoffrey. 'It's a f#@%ing horse race.'

He slammed the car into reverse, narrowly missing a parked car in his haste to escape the thundering equines. We were speechless; not so our Marjorie who continued to command Geoffrey to maintain his course and stop divvying[1] about like an idiot.

'Shut that thing up,' commanded Geoffrey.

As soon as we were clear of the melee, we parked up next to the Rhône River for Geoffrey to calm his beating pulse.

As we scouted around, there was no sign of hotels anywhere and it was now getting dark. Onwards we headed to the next town marked on the map, Nîmes, where we turned off and began a grid search of the place. We didn't know where we were going so Marjorie slumped into silence. The kids started to nod off in the back seat but were jerked awake by their father shouting, 'Shit, shit, shit, it's a one-way street.'

They watched with interest as the oncoming car's headlights inched past us with the occupants leaning out, threatening us with some sort of French torture. Geoffrey became apoplectic; apparently it was my fault for bringing us to France and not learning the French road signs. As we passed another one-way street, I noticed the big red sign saying *INTERDIT*.

'I wonder what that means?' I asked.

'It means don't flipping go down there,' said smart-arse Geoffrey.

Jan helpfully Googled it. 'Forbidden or prohibited is the answer you're looking for, Mum. That's what those barriers said where you drove into the horse race, Dad,' she added.

'Well isn't this great; we've all learnt a new French word today,' I said. '*Interdit.*'

Onwards we rolled until finally on the outskirts of Montpellier at 10:30 p.m., we spotted a dodgy-looking autoroute hotel at a service area on the other side of the highway. It was a dirty, disgusting, flea-ridden, overpriced dump but we were too knackered to care. Welcome to France and *bonne nuit* (goodnight).

---

1. Dithering.

THE BLOOD BATH

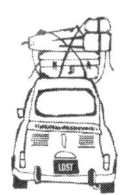

What a dump. Not the autoroute hotel, which was as bad as it looked. I mean the house we'd just arrived at in Durban-Corbières in the Aude department of Southern France. The pictures on TripAdvisor didn't do it justice. They made it look lovely; it was, in fact, dire. In fairness we didn't get off to the most auspicious start. Following the house instructions, we arrived at a long, narrow alley where we promptly got stuck with no way of turning around. Marjorie the satnav and the house instructions said we'd arrived; however there was no house sign or numbers outside any of the homes. We re-read the owner's notes and they definitely said the name of the place was on a plaque outside as well as the house number. The website photos didn't include an outside shot so we had nothing to go on as unfortunately we aren't psychic.

Thankfully a kind lady came out of her home and knew which property we were looking for—a regular occurrence perhaps? She walked behind the car, carefully guiding Geoffrey in as he reversed back along the narrow alley to the correct house. The off-street parking turned out to be a case of 'pull your wing mirrors in and park one inch from the stone wall'. Not to worry; we were there now and it was 30 degrees so we needed to get out of the hot car and indoors. We started dragging our bags up the steps into the little courtyard where the key was to be under the lantern. But no, of course not. There was the lantern, but no key. We scouted the tiny garden on the off-chance there was another lantern, but no.

I had to make an expensive phone call to the owner in the UK who said he would send Celine, the local cleaning lady, down with the key for us. She was supposed to have been in and cleaned then left the key under the lantern. We sat down in the garden to wait and the kids started moaning. Finally Celine arrived and let us in, telling us the people who'd just left had accidentally taken the garage key with them so we wouldn't be able to access the garage to park or use the washing machine, bikes, BBQ or sun umbrella.

OK then. I guess we can sit on the deck in our dirty clothes and fry under the hot sun. Hopefully there was a good kitchen so we would be fine without a BBQ.

Celine left us to it and scarpered, not surprising given the state of the place. I suspect she was taking the money from the owner for cleaning but doing as little as humanly possible. However, we couldn't hold her responsible for the lack of general maintenance and broken or missing amenities. The old French house was on three levels, which was fine; however, the photos hadn't shown the stairs between them. The first staircase was at least solid, albeit a tight, very steep spiral with narrow steps and no handrail. The second staircase, which we nicknamed the stairway of death, was a barely-there corkscrew of rickety wooden treads loosely attached to a central pole. This led to the kids' bedroom on the top floor.

The house layout wasn't user-friendly with just one toilet on the bottom level. Imagine having to traverse both those sets of dangerous stairs in the night to go to the loo. The tiny, good-for-nothing kitchen was on the bottom level but the dining room was up the steep spiral stairs. I could just picture us all trying to balance our plates of food and drink while gingerly negotiating the tight and narrow spiral.

We should get danger money to stay here, I thought. *It's a death trap.*

I surveyed the scene with dismay. The kitchen sink was a bucket under a faucet dangling from the wall; there was a gas-top stove with only one hob; no oven, nowhere to hang a tea towel or hand towel and half the crockery and cookware was broken or missing. There was no bench at all on which to prepare food, just a little tray table, so it was next to impossible to produce a meal for four. The toilet had a tiny, hand-washing sink in it with the towel rack lying broken on the floor. The floor itself was disgusting; there was that much dust, dirt and human hair piled up around all four walls of the room that it looked like sand dunes.

Anyway, I digress. Geoffrey started the difficult challenge of getting the kids' suitcases up their terrifying spiral staircase. It wasn't long before he was bellowing in pain and swearing; he'd managed to bend his glasses into his eye socket. Ouch. While unpacking, I stabbed my leg on the sharp, wooden edge of the bed base that stuck out. Shit, it hurt. I threw myself down onto the bed to recover. Thrummmppp. I was left winded; it was as hard as a rock. I climbed the stairs of doom to tell Geoffrey I reckoned I'd dislocated my shoulder but as I reached the top I heard an almighty scream and saw him hopping on one foot, clutching the other as blood spurted from it.

'Shit!' he yelled. 'I've stabbed myself on the plug trying to get this goddamn internet working.' He hopped to the couch and sat down.

'Get up, get up,' I screamed. 'It's white leather. You can't bleed there!'

Geoffrey hobbled off to the bathroom to bleed all over the shower floor while I hunted for our first aid kit. Jan and Don were looking down from the top of their spiral staircase.

'I think it's haunted,' said Jan.

'Nah, it's the gypsy curse,' claimed Don.

'Shut up,' yelled their father from the shower.

'No one's cursed,' I insisted.

Once Geoffrey's plug-imprinted foot was suitably covered, I decided to have a shower and get rid of the blood at the same time. I chuckled to myself while in there. Talk about a blood bath. My mirth didn't last long. The water wasn't draining away and soon spread in a red-tinged tsunami across the entire bathroom floor and under the doorway. I had to cut my shower short, leap out and run screaming for everyone to bring towels to stem the flow before it reached the carpet.

'Is this what they call a red tide?' asked smarty-pants Don.

'No, and don't even think about mentioning gypsies. I'm not in the mood.'

We had to call Celine who rang for a plumber. While we waited for him to arrive, Jan went upstairs to finish unpacking. As she hung her coat on a wooden rack, it fell off the wall and whacked her. She came downstairs clutching her bleeding head and needed the first aid kit.

'Jeez,' groaned Geoffrey. 'I'm beginning to think this place *is* haunted.'

Just then there was a shout from downstairs. Don had jammed his finger in the faulty toilet door lock.

'Unbelievable,' muttered Geoffrey.

There was a knock at the door and Monsieur Plumber arrived to remove all the greasy hair left behind in the shower drain by the previous guests. He took in the scene before him: blood-stained water, Jan's bleeding head, Don's bleeding finger and Geoffrey's bandaged foot. That man worked at the speed of light and was out of there even faster, with a furtive look over his shoulder as he left the house. I bet we were the talk of the village next day. With injuries dressed, everyone headed to bed and I prayed no one would fall down the stairs in the night.

Now some of you might be thinking, 'They can't possibly have had that many accidents in the space of an hour. She's making that up.' Well let me reassure you, I'm writing this directly from my handwritten travel journal which I write daily on all of our trips. Sadly it's all true.

A couple of days later while visiting Carcassonne, a medieval, walled fortress and UNESCO World Heritage town, we decided to visit the Museum of the Inquisition against those accused of witchcraft, followed by a visit to the haunted house. Given all that had been going on in our accommodation, this may not have been the wisest choice of activity but the kids were keen so in we went. After paying our money, we and our fellow guests waited for the door to open then in we went into complete, and I mean complete, blackness. No French health and safety rules here; no fluorescent light strips or lit-up exit signs. No, sir, we were left huddled together in the darkness, not sure who or what we were touching and trying not to hold the hand of a stranger while praying the floor was level and without hidden stairs. One thing was certain: if there were stairs, one of my family would be first to find them and fall.

Oh, but wait. There *were* stairs—a spiral stone staircase heading down into a dungeon. A voice shouted at us to get down there pronto before the door on a timer shut. The people at the head of the queue located the stairs and we all shuffled close together, holding onto the person in front while we felt our way gingerly down. Then the fun began with mad Frenchmen leaping out from the shadows, screaming at us. Don, Jan and another lady yelled back. In fact they screamed and screamed, turning into quivering, limpet-like jellies, clinging onto me.

As we moved through the house, a voice would yell at us that we only had twenty seconds to get through each doorway before it shut. Of course no one wanted to be separated from the group and left behind in the dark alone so that freaked everyone out. Don and Jan were petrified at the thought so surged through the next door first then promptly froze in fear, blocking the entry for the rest of us. Strangers in the dark grabbed their hands and took them. One of the strangers was the other screaming lady so they all clung together. I was surprised by the kids' apparent fear given that they'd begged to come in and normally loved scary books and movies. They did laugh about it later though.

When we reached the exit, a crazed ghoul chased us out into the alleyway, with the screamers screaming and me laughing my head off. Now that was what I call fun. I wanted to do it again but no way were Don and Jan going back in there so we had crêpes with strawberries and apricots for lunch instead.

A week later the happy day finally arrived when we could leave Durban-Corbières and our own house of horrors behind forever, hoping never to return. I was by now trained in the culinary art of one-pot cooking and how to use chairs as extra bench space. The kids could pass as wait staff in the finest of Parisian cafés with their new-found skills at delicately balancing plates and dishes while traversing corkscrew staircases with finesse. And Geoffrey, well he managed a whole week without reversing into the stone wall while parking. We thought about making him a certificate.

After driving for 30 minutes, Geoffrey suddenly shouted, 'Oh shit,' and turned the car around. The kids pulled their earphones out and looked at him.

'Where are we going?' I asked.

'Durban-Corbières.'

'What? Why?' We all groaned.

'I left €900 under Don's mattress,' confessed Geoffrey.

'Why did you put money under my mattress?' asked Don.

'To keep it safe.'

'Wonder if the cleaner found it,' I speculated.

'Shit,' said Geoffrey and put his foot down.

'She could be on her way to Monte Carlo,' I added.

As we screeched up to the house, Celine hadn't departed for Monte Carlo yet. She'd just left the place and was walking up the street, cleaning bucket in hand and hopefully not an apron full of cash. Geoffrey sprinted after her, shouting, '*Bonjour, bonjour.* I need to get in the house.'

We all watched and sniggered.

'Dad sounds so stupid,' said Jan as she and Don mimicked him, calling, '*Bonjour, bonjour,*' in a sing-song voice.

Geoffrey returned a few minutes later, wallet bulging. 'Right, let's get out of this shithole,' he announced and we headed off on a new adventure. I made a mental note to restock the first aid kit in case we actually were cursed.

P.S. While sitting in a restaurant having lunch in Levanto, Italy, a couple of weeks later, one of Geoffrey's lenses fell out of his glasses onto his plate. I can't tell you how funny that was. The stairway of death had struck again. Geoffrey spent the afternoon ringing our insurance company and getting new glasses while we spent his money. A win-win.

THE SAUSAGE ESCAPADE

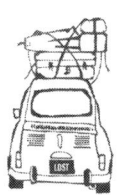

We were now staying in Peschici on the Gargano Peninsula in the southeast of Italy where we had a top-floor apartment with an outdoor balcony overlooking the Adriatic Sea and the whitewashed houses below. We were going to be there for a week and after being kept awake by a neighbouring dog's incessant barking for the first two nights, we took matters into our own hands.

From the balcony we could see the offending canine: a large bulldog chained up on a small, outside patio. The poor thing didn't move from this spot, which must've been very boring, so at night when the local felines came out to prowl, he started his deep-throated, baritone WOOF. Geoffrey was dispatched to the butcher's to fetch some sausages. The plan was to feed the dog lots of them so he had a good night's sleep and hopefully so would we.

After our dinner of sausages, we waited for the sun to go down and watched our canine friend pacing the length of his chain in boredom. *That's all about to change, my friend*, I mentally said to him. *Tonight's the night that flying sausages will come sailing through the air to land at your feet. We just have to try not to get caught.*

Once it was suitably dark, we assembled on our terrace, armed with the sausages. The kids were assigned to keep watch. It seemed like a great idea at the time but now we were having doubts. What if we got caught? Our balcony had a solid, waist-height edge so we kept low as we got in position. Geoffrey had the best hand-eye coordination; he took aim and let the first sausage fly across the alley and two floors below. It hit the target with a thump. The bulldog was startled, looking all around, but then spied the sausage and gulped it down in one. We ducked down below the balustrade, doubled over with quiet mirth. The kids checked the coast was clear before Geoffrey let rip with another flying sausage. It landed with a thwack. The bulldog was alert and couldn't quite believe his luck as yet another sausage appeared before him. This was going splendidly.

Geoffrey launched sausage number three but to our horror it landed with a loud smack on the tiled roof of the porch. The outside light came on and we heard the door being unlocked. We crouched down quickly, smothering our laughter with our hands. I had to crawl inside on my hands and knees. I thought I was going to wet myself. Don peeked over the edge. The house owner looked all around, puzzled by what had made the noise. Finally he retreated indoors and turned the light out again. Geoffrey had lost his bravado but I wanted a turn; after all, the dog had only had two sausages. I wasn't sure that was enough to sustain him through the night.

Of course I had no coordination or strength. I took aim and threw and the sausage sailed straight down below us to land with a smack on the neighbour's glass conservatory roof. I gasped in horror; there was the offending sausage lying clearly visible below us. Surely the house owners only had to look up to figure out where the food could have come from. We scooted shamefaced inside and turned out our lights.

The following day dawned bright and sunny and we sat down to breakfast on our terrace. There below us the sausage sat in all its glory on the glass as proof of foul play. I prayed for a huge seagull to land and eat the evidence before it was discovered. Suddenly the neighbours entered their conservatory, carrying a tray of coffee. I froze. We quickly gathered up our breakfast things to move inside but our movements caught their eye and they looked up to wave. Only now they weren't looking at us; their eyes were firmly fixed on the strange apparition of a sausage on their roof. We made ourselves scarce and lived with the guilt for the rest of the week.

Oh, and the bulldog slept well that night.

2014

GREECE, FRANCE, ITALY, CROATIA, BOSNIA AND HERZEGOVINA, AND THE UAE

PATIENCE, MADAM. WE'RE TAKING YOU TO THE SPECIAL NEEDS LOUNGE

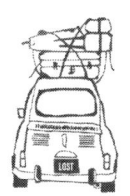

I was sitting in a wheelchair in the special needs lounge at Dubai International Airport. Geoffrey was pleased that my moon boot had gained us comfortable chairs, newspapers and magazines and he was sprawled out with his nose in the paper. Never mind the fact that I'd just been labelled special needs, much to the snickering amusement of my children. I didn't imagine for a moment that they were going to let me forget that in a hurry. They were busy tapping away on their devices; Jan on her iPad, Don on his phone, no doubt both gleefully announcing to the Facebook world that their mother was special needs. Who *says* that? It's not even politically correct but I guess it was meant as 'special needs within transit'. Geoffrey had his laptop bag beside him, making me the only one without technology. Our family don't do 'travelling light'; hence the gadgets and their associated cords, chargers and adaptors had a bag of their own.

We were heading off on another family adventure, starting our trip in Greece, so we'd be flying into Athens then heading out to Santorini for a week followed by a week in a small mountain village in the Peloponnese. If we made it through the first two weeks without killing each other, we'd continue to France, Italy and Croatia for the remainder of the three months.

I guess I should explain why I'd found myself in the special needs lounge wearing a most fetching black moonboot, an orthopaedic boot to stabilise a foot or ankle injury. I'll try to keep it short. I was injured by Thomas the Tank Engine. I stepped on him at work in bare feet and tore a tendon.

'What did you do to your foot?' one of the children at the kindergarten asked.

'I stood on Thomas.'

He looked me up and down slowly, taking in my bulky shape before asking, 'How's Thomas?'

After eighteen months of medical to-ing and fro-ing, it was decided that an operation was necessary. This happened to be three months before we intended to go to Europe so its timing was rather closer to departure than ideal. Hence I headed off with strict instructions from my physio and a raft of ugly, sensible shoes padded up with orthotics from the orthopaedic specialist. The surgeon told me I was to avoid cobblestones and wasn't allowed anywhere near a beach unless my foot and ankle were totally wrapped in surgical tape. Seriously? So apart from the bagful of gadgets and my fan collection, we had one bag just for the moonboot, walking stick, surgical tape and hideous, big, black, clunky, old lady shoes.

The surgeon's words had echoed in my head as I packed. 'Under no circumstances are you to wear those flimsy Crocs or Skechers.' I guiltily popped both into my suitcase. Along with the bags, we had four large suitcases, four maximum-sized cabin bags, two handbags, one backpack and a laptop bag. All of this was joined later by bags of groceries. In short, practically a travelling circus, which is pretty much what we were.

My doctor recommended I ask for wheelchair assistance at the airport as it wasn't long since my operation. I hadn't had time to heal or even start walking properly after a month spent learning the finer points of using a Zimmer frame and crutches. I was horrified and refused. But having thought about it, I decided to accept the assistance in Dubai no matter how embarrassing it was as I knew from experience that it was a difficult airport to negotiate with long queues.

As we stepped off the plane, there was my wheelchair waiting for me, along with a porter or whatever you call someone who very kindly carts around heavy loads. The poor man was only a wee slip of a thing. I felt like I should pop him in the chair and push *him*. It was my first time in a wheelchair and I was mortified. I felt like people were looking at me and thinking I was just too lazy to walk. Once I was in the chair, he whisked Geoffrey, the kids and me off, skirting all the public areas and taking us behind the scenes using a myriad of corridors and lifts that bypassed all the queues. He then took us to a private security check area for the aged and infirm, away from the general public. The staff on duty here were unsmiling and abrupt. I deliberately smiled brightly and said, 'Good morning,' just to annoy them. No response. 'Are you having a great day?' I asked, all saccharine smiles. No response. 'It's been a pleasure meeting you,' I added.

Geoffrey shot me a warning look; he knows me too well. He's the peacemaker, but with a terrible temper, and I'm the naughty one. I kept my mouth shut. Little did I know that I would be forced to grovel shamelessly to the Arabs on the return journey to save us from being thrown in jail.

We were handed over, along with our boarding passes, to a holding pen for the transit-disabled with some other inmates and told to wait. Three hours we spent there with no access to food or water. The woman behind the desk was no help at all, telling me very sternly, 'Patience, madam.' After doing time, we were granted a pardon and released then led away to an electric car which whizzed us through the crowds at a rapid pace; it was awesome. The kids were thrilled at getting to ride on one of these airport vehicles and were pleased that my moonboot was literally opening doors for them. We sped through the terminal at high speed with the driver honking the horn at anyone in his way.

One of the inmates, an elderly lady who'd obviously been to the same school of patience as me, got a strop on, demanding coffee and food.

'I'm sick of this carry-on,' she snapped at the driver.

'Patience, madam,' he replied. 'We're taking you all to the special needs lounge.'

My eyes widened. We all exchanged looks and I mouthed, 'SPECIAL NEEDS.' The kids sniggered mercilessly at their mother's new title. We came to a halt and a flotilla of porters with wheelchairs met us. Into a final wheelchair I went and then we were ceremoniously admitted to the luxurious special needs lounge where someone told us to wait.

So there I was, shortly to be wheeled to the door of the plane and allowed to board before everyone else. Who'd have thought my foot would be our ticket to the front of all queues? No wonder Geoffrey was lapping it up. It would probably be the only time we'd ever be let into a private lounge at an airport. We're very definitely not private-lounge material.

When the time came to board, we were escorted to a crowded departure lounge. My family was able to anonymously join the masses and sit on the floor while I and my new best friend the wheelchair were deposited up at the front alone, ready to go on first. The porter applied the brake and I found myself parked facing a staring sea of faces, all looking at me with a degree of suspicion or open hostility for my queue-jumping, wily ways.

Well, this isn't one bit awkward, I thought, wishing I could disappear. *Being labelled 'special needs' in transit terms has its downsides.* I blushed as I imagined what they might be thinking: 'Look at that fat tart, too lazy to walk.' This impression wasn't helped by the fact that once on board, I ripped the moonboot off and tossed it into the overhead locker. I had to endure a few withering looks after that. But I decided they could think what they liked and I wasn't going to justify myself to everyone. But for you, readers, I will explain: the moonboot really was needed to give my foot support and stability if I was required to walk any distance or on uneven ground. But as far as my fellow travellers were concerned, I was a queue-jumping fraud. Happy days.

NOT FOR THE UNATTRACTIVE

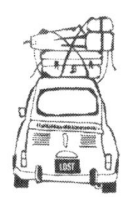

I might add to the title description that Santorini isn't for people who can't stand the heat either but it was at least a dry heat, tempered by the gale-force winds blowing in off the Aegean Sea. After a ferry ride from Athens, we arrived at the Greek port of Firá, the capital of Santorini, on a sweltering and windy day to commence the sweaty job of dragging all our bags off the ferry onto the bustling wharf. We were instantaneously absorbed into a world of noise, heat and movement as we were swept along in the tide of moving bodies. The local police were blowing so hard on their whistles, it's a wonder they could get enough oxygen. They were tasked with the frustrating job of trying to keep the passengers from straying into the path of the offloading and onloading vehicles. I didn't envy them as the sensory overload rendered most tourists dumbstruck and they wandered around completely oblivious.

A posse of brochure- and sign-waving travel reps, car- and scooter-rental companies met us, all trying to out-shout one another. The tour buses and guides herded their groups together and we found Tony from Tony's Car Rentals holding up a sign with our name on it. We followed him to our car then joined the queue of traffic heading up the switchback road hugging the rim of the caldera cliff. The coloured layers of volcanic strata in red and black contrasting with the stark white of the clifftop houses and the blue of the sea and sky struck me immediately. My travel fatigue was instantly replaced by a sense of wonderment and my jetlag and tiredness from the early start evaporated. This of course had been alleviated by four iced coffees on board the ferry. Welcome to Santorini, the largest of the Cyclades islands.

Once we had the car sorted, we followed the directions to Pyrgos, the largest preserved village on Santorini and the island's former capital, at the highest point on the island, with views reaching to Oia. Pyrgos is a typical fortress settlement of the Cyclades featuring traditional architecture of tiny, whitewashed houses along narrow, winding lanes leading up to Kastelli Castle at the top. Donkeys are still used to deliver goods, groceries and building supplies around the village as the lanes are too narrow for cars.

Following the instructions from the house owner, we duly arrived at the designated spot. The website had said the house was a short, easy walk from the car. Geoffrey treated this with a healthy degree of scepticism given past experiences. The holiday rental representative was there to meet us and take us to our accommodation. She was a Swiss woman as lithe and agile as a mountain goat and she bounded off in the lead. We all looked at where she was going and Geoffrey muttered, 'And I wonder who's expected to get our luggage up there?'

'Well don't include me in that. I'm "special needs", remember,' said I, grabbing my walking stick and handbag and hobbling after her with a rather overly pronounced limp.

My three porters struggled along behind with the luggage while I panted after the Swiss mountain goat. What was wrong with the woman? Couldn't she slow down a bit? The route did level out after the initial very steep bit though was mostly uphill and it was scorchingly hot. We were on the lower slope of the village, walking along a donkey path. I could tell that by the piles of donkey poo and hoped that it didn't end up in the wheels of my suitcase. I wouldn't have put it past Geoffrey to roll my case through it deliberately in revenge.

Finally we arrived at a small, whitewashed house and entered a gate into a central courtyard. The place was breathtaking: a traditional, stone, artisan home, lovingly restored and complete with stone floors with a glass-covered opening in the floor where you could see down to the well below. The porters soon forgave me once they saw the rooftop terrace with the amazing view over the island and out to sea. Above us was the castle wall and stretching out below was a view of Firá, and Oia in the distance, perched along the clifftop.

There was just one downside to all the whitewashed bliss—toileting. The Swiss goat lady informed us that we couldn't flush paper down the toilet on this island.

'No, you mean we can't flush sanitary items; don't worry, we wouldn't do that,' I assured her.

'No, you can't flush *any* paper down the toilet at all,' she emphasised.

That got our attention. Four pairs of eyes widened and stared at her, trying to grasp what we were supposed to do after wiping our bums.

'You put the paper in the bin,' she explained.

'What? So we're going to have a bin full of poo?' I asked.

Yep, we were, and guess who had to tie it up and empty it each morning? That's right—yours truly. Then I had to carry it down the track back to the bins by the car. It became known as the "poo-'n-'ere" bag. I found it gross that you still had to put your hand in a bin full of strangers' poo and pee in restaurants and tourist places. I was delighted that I'd made us get hepatitis A shots before we left home. I noted to myself that we needed to find hand sanitiser at the earliest opportunity.

I quickly unpacked my cooling fans and put them to good use; the swivel fan that I had blowing on me all night meant the mozzies got caught in the crosswind and blown onto Geoffrey where they crash-landed with a readymade meal. He woke up every morning covered in bites and wondering why. The kids were also covered in bites and I had none; that would teach them to be so rude about my fans.

Jan brought me some Kathmandu cooling strips that you soak in water then wrap around you. I sat writing my travel diary with one around my head, another around my neck and my feet in a bucket of icy cold water. Don said I looked like a deranged ninja. Inside the walls of our ancient villa, it stayed at a constant temperature of 26.5 degrees, about 10 degrees warmer than my ideal. But hey, it was August in Greece and I was happy dealing with the heat in my own way. I looked weird but that was OK too.

Oia, as predicted, was the picture-perfect postcard scene that everyone recognises when they think of Greece: the blue-domed churches, white buildings and bougainvillea cascading down the cliff to a beautiful blue sea. From below it looked like a lot of enormous birds had pooed all over the top of the cliff.

What the guidebooks don't tell you is that everyone looks like a Hollywood starlet or a model straight off the pages of *Vogue*. Male and female, all looked like gods and goddesses gliding around, tall, willowy, muscly, tanned and dressed to kill in haute couture accessorised with stilettos, bags draped over an arm, matching designer sunglasses and parasols, diamonds glinting in the sun. Unless you have a hefty dose of self-esteem then this place is probably not for you.

And then there was us: Geoffrey with his beer belly, flip flops, dirty and wrinkled shorts and T-shirt and me in my overweight, middle-aged-mother's uniform of three-quarter pants and top. All four of us a pasty-white colour. Jan looked better than the rest of us but it was impossible to measure up against these standards; she charged off to find just the right overpriced designer outfit and as for me, I simply didn't care. Even outside of touristy Oia, on the roads you couldn't escape the beautiful men driving around on quad bikes and scooters with bare, tanned, muscle-bound torsos and dark glasses, black hair waving in the wind (not that I noticed that much). The accessory of choice was a gorgeous-figured, bikini-clad girl on the back, helmets extraneous. It was all about the look and a designer beach bag slung casually over the girl's arm, hinting at a long and romantic day in the sun. Then I sniggered. They might be rich, famous or just gorgeous but they still had to use the "poo-'n-'ere" bag like the rest of us.

Embracing our lack of chic, we marched into a boutique spa therapy shop, which the Kardashians had visited, as Jan and Don wanted to try a fish spa. Jan convinced Geoffrey that he should have a go too. Of course the spa was full of beautiful people and then there was us. *Suck it up, people; you'll just have to put on your fat and dishevelled filters.* After Geoffrey, Jan and Don had scrubbed up their legs, they lowered them into their individual aquariums full of starving, toe-jam-deprived fish.

The creatures went into a feeding frenzy, especially on Geoffrey's filthy and dead skin. It was a pity we couldn't have put his shorts in there as well for a damn good cleaning. The fish gnawed away; the kids shrieked and laughed while I and my hideously un-couture-like bandaged foot lounged next to the air con, which turned out to be the best on the island. Don forgot he had to keep his feet off the bottom.

'Mum,' he whispered, 'I've accidentally killed a fish under my feet.'

'Don't worry. The others will probably eat its body in a flash; no one will know.'

Too late, the spa attendant snapped at him to be careful. To say we lowered the tone of the spa would be an understatement. At my time of life, I'm way beyond caring what people think of me, which is very liberating really as it frees you up to be a bit naughty.

Despite being someone who doesn't like boats, I had for some reason booked a sunset cruise on a small boat for Jan's 21st birthday. I'd Googled and researched photos of the vessel to reassure myself that I could clamber aboard it without tipping myself overboard. I also emailed the captain and told him I would have a moonboot on and asked if that would be a problem. His reply was about ordering a birthday cake and the weather so I assumed I was good to go. I didn't realise that being Greek, he didn't understand what I was asking.

We arrived at the dock at the appointed hour and stood beside the little boat which was rocking up and down in the choppy waters. Captain Savros looked at my moonboot and said in a somewhat accusatory fashion, 'No one tells me about thisssss. You cannot come on my boat.'

Happy Birthday, Jan.

Banned from the boat, we went back up the cable car to a fancy and pricey-looking clifftop restaurant with a fantastic view. Jan ordered a very flash cocktail and took an appreciative sip. The donkeys came clip-clopping past on their way up the hill and Jan leapt up to take a photo. She forgot we were on a raised platform and promptly fell off, doing a great impersonation of mid-air swimming, but managed to stay upright. She wasn't hurt and I managed not to laugh out loud. Jan returned to her cocktail. This was when her brother hissed, 'Mum, I've got the shits. We have to go.'

'Oh my God. It's probably hepatitis,' I speculated.

'But my cocktail,' moaned Jan. 'Can't I just finish it?'

The answer was apparent as Don shot off down the path towards the car and Geoffrey paid the waiter. Not exactly the 21st I'd envisioned.

Later that evening we realised Captain Savros was sailing around the island feasting on Jan's special birthday cake. She didn't speak to us for the rest of the night.

We decided (well, *they* did) we wanted to do a boat ride out to the volcanic island of Nea Kameni to see the active crater and walk around the rim but once again I would need a gangplank for easy access to the boat. Geoffrey and Jan popped into a travel agent in the town to arrange it and Geoffrey promised he would make sure I had what I needed. The ladies in the travel agent didn't speak much English. Once they'd established which cruise he wanted, he asked about access to the boat for the disabled.

They weren't sure what he meant by disabled so came around from the counter for a game of charades. They went first, miming out someone in a wheelchair. Geoffrey shook his head. They mimed out a Zimmer frame. Nope. Geoffrey pretended to be a pirate, shouting,

'Ahoy, me hearties,' and hobbled up a make-believe gangplank, holding onto the sides with a pronounced limp.

'Ahhh, no problem,' they said. 'Yes, yes, she will be fine, sir. Not a problem.'

Geoffrey's pirate imitation mortified Jan. He proudly reported back to me that it was all sorted, mission accomplished.

The tour bus delivered the party of tourists to the wharf and there was a small and rusty boat and a one-metre jump onto a boat lurching up and down.

'Geoffrey, where's the gangplank?' I demanded with a note of hysteria.

Everyone got on board and looked at me expectantly then at my taped-up foot and ankle. *Shit*, I thought. *I can't back out now they're all waiting and watching for my display of natural balance and agility, of which I have neither.* I inched forward, imagining myself being crushed to death between the boat and the wharf when I fell in. Then two Greek gods grabbed me. I closed my eyes tight and when I opened them, I was on board. *Oh, well, still alive, off we go then.*

We sailed out to the volcano where you could climb up to the top on a surface of crumbly pumice and lava rock. I stayed on the boat, enjoying the scenery. The others returned, red in the face and sweating.

'What was it like?' I asked.

'Cool,' replied Don.

'Just a pile of rocks,' Jan said.

Fair comment from where I was sitting.

Next we sailed to the island of Palia Kameni where some offshore, volcanic hot springs bubbled up near the beach, giving the water a vivid, yellowy-green colour. Geoffrey and Jan leapt in and swam the 30 metres to the shore to reach the springs. Don, who wasn't a confident swimmer, stayed on board with me on shark-spotting duty.

However, a young Asian man on our boat diverted my attention as he emerged in his togs, looking very nervous, and asked the captain if there was a boat to take him over to the beach. *Errr, no, you leap in and swim if you can. This could be interesting*, I thought, and nudged Don in the ribs then repositioned myself to where I could see better. The young Asian gentleman paced up and down the stern of the sailing boat, looking petrified. The deckhand had hopped in the water and was floating on a rescue ring some distance away; he too watched and waited. The young man leapt in and sank. We craned our heads over the side, following his downward progress with concern. Finally he re-emerged, doing the underwater ladder climb of the drowning, and reached out. Thankfully someone grabbed his arm and pulled him back on board. He learnt a valuable lesson that day: if you can't swim at home, being on holiday doesn't give you magic powers.

I got back to my shark-spotting duties, quietly confident that there were so many other bodies thrashing around in the water that one of them was bound to be eaten before my family, giving them time to escape.

After a week of hot weather, iced coffees, beautiful people, donkeys, delicious local red wine and amazing sunsets, it was time to move on. I hoped where we went next had a healthy dose of unattractive people. I would feel so much better.

LOST IN THE PELOPONNESE

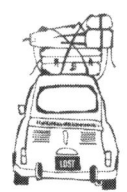

Well, changeover day was an epic and stressful event (who would've thought it?) so sit back with a cuppa and enjoy. We arrived back at Piraeus port in Athens after a very smooth sailing from Santorini. I felt quietly confident that this changeover day would go well; after all, I'd said a few silent prayers and was practising thinking positive thoughts so what could go wrong?

The car rental man met us off the ship and led us at a brisk pace to the car. When I say brisk, I mean brisk for him as he wasn't trying to drag four large suitcases, four cabin bags, two handbags, a laptop bag, a backpack, a bag of groceries and the moonboot. Nor did he deem it necessary to offer to lighten our load.

When we caught up with him at the car, I studied him with interest and couldn't help comparing him to one of my mother's typically untrue and unfounded stereotypes—the greasy Greek. I watched as sweat poured off him, dribbling down his face and neck as he produced a small towel and used it every few minutes to mop the liquid oozing from him. *Yeah, it's hot,* I thought, whipping Singapore fan out of my handbag. The kids were already in the car and ready to go. Geoffrey signed the paperwork and asked about the satnav. The man pulled a little gadget out of the glove box and plugged it into the cigarette lighter. *Oh no,* I thought. *What's that?* It produced a miniature map with very little else. The man gave very scant instructions in a heavily accented voice and tried to leave. I detained him with a rising sense of panic, questioning him about how to get out of the port and to the autoroute.

'Just go left and follow the signs,' he said. 'You can't get lost.'

Want to bet?

Geoffrey examined the poor excuse for a satnav and programmed it for where we wanted to go. We left the port, turned left and 150 metres later we were lost in the bustling port of Piraeus. 'Follow the signs,' the man had said. Well, he didn't add that after the first sign there wouldn't be another with our destination or road number on it; each intersection became a guessing game. 'Why weren't you following the satnav?' I hear you ask. Well, because that piece of rubbish was the reason we'd gone astray. With her shrill and commanding voice ordering us to enter one-way streets the wrong way and leading us down a myriad of alleyways, she got us completely and hopelessly lost. Difficult enough in a car you're familiar with let alone one you climbed into a few minutes previously. It had only taken a few minutes before Geoffrey shoved the satnav at me.

'Just make her stop,' he groaned.

I had no idea how to turn the satnav off so opted to yank her plug out. She was christened Marjorie for the remainder of our time in Greece, just like her counterpart in Nice.

There was now absolute silence in the car. The tension was almost unbearable as we waited for Geoffrey to have a meltdown. On the positive side of things, driving down the tight alleyways gave us a good close-up look at how washing can be strung across the street and along the balconies.

'It's just like that time Dad nearly drove us onto the ship going to Africa,' said Don.

'Oh yeah, I'd forgotten about that,' Jan replied. 'We were driving through slums just like this, with washing everywhere.'

'Then everyone started screaming at us to get out because we were going the wrong way down that street and Dad had a fit.'

They burst out laughing and Geoffrey shouted at them to shut up. They were referring to an incident that happened in Castellammare, Italy, where we weren't even supposed to be. After the one-way street fiasco and mad Italians rightfully yelling at him, Geoffrey lost confidence and decided just to follow another vehicle; that way he wouldn't accidentally make the same mistake. So he'd followed a truck; great plan, except the vehicle was driving onto the wharf and a ferry bound for North Africa. As you can imagine, finding ourselves in a lane queuing to board a ship caused Geoffrey no end of angst and a substantial amount of panicked F-bombing. As if extricating ourselves from the ship queue wasn't bad enough, we were then left bouncing our way around the wooden wharf, dodging giant ropes, ferry workers and freight as we tried to find a way off. And you guessed it, more people waving and shouting at us. It was so embarrassing.

Anyway, back to Athens. Eventually Geoffrey got us out of the narrow alleyways and onto a sort of main-looking road again with the slim possibility of seeing another signpost at some point. We found the autoroute and began heading in the right direction towards the Peloponnese and our destination of a village called Vrousti. We stopped for dinner at an autoroute services. It was 33 degrees and clouds were gathering both out of the car and within.

We somehow took a wrong exit and instead of bypassing Corinth on the autoroute, we ended up driving through it. I started explaining to the kids about the Corinth Canal which separates the Gulf of Corinth in the Ionian Sea with the Saronic Gulf in the Aegean Sea. We drove over a bridge and I looked down.

'Oh, that was it,' I said as we reached the other side. No one saw it and no one cared.

'This place is shit,' moaned Don.

'Are we lost?' asked Jan, yanking her headphones out of her ears temporarily.

'No, we're on a detour,' I lied.

Just then an electrical storm broke and it started to get dark. We managed to get back onto the autoroute and find the correct exit. All was going well again.

This was when we noticed that someone really didn't like English-speaking tourists in the Peloponnese as they'd taken the time to spray-paint over all signposts that had the English version on them, leaving just the Greek, not exactly invoking thoughts of a warm welcome. I was inwardly panicking as it was nearly dark and pelting with rain; the satnav didn't work; the signs were in Greek and we only had some notes from the houseowner to follow.

We also needed food as the supermarkets would be shut next day as it was Sunday. Our notes from the house owner said the supermarket nearest to the house in Argos closed at 8 p.m. We reached it at 8:15 p.m. and saw lights on and people still inside. We screeched to a halt and ran. The entrance doors were shut. Damn. We hovered by the exit and as soon as someone came out, we all dashed in. I yelled out, 'Split and grab what you can,' and rushed to the wine aisle while the kids headed to the ice cream section. Luckily Geoffrey thought of things like bread and milk.

So, we were in Argos—tick. We had food—tick. Now all we had to do was find the turnoff which would take us out of town to our village. But could we see it? No. We later discovered that the very signpost we were blindly searching for in the dark had been removed for roadworks and just never replaced; a fact that wasn't updated in the houseowner's notes. It was on about our fourth reconnaissance through Argos that Geoffrey's cork finally popped.

'What do these people have against bloody signposts?' he shouted. 'They're either invisible or covered in goddamn spray paint. Right, we're going down this road; it has to be it and if it's not then it's too bad,' he thundered.

'We're hungry,' moaned the kids.

'Eat your ice cream then; it's going to melt anyway,' I snapped.

'We don't have spoons,' they chorused.

'Use your tongues then. It will stop you moaning.'

Silence reigned, apart from the thunder. We left behind all the lights of the town and headed into nowhere. We drove on and on and on, pausing at crossroads and shining a torch on our instructions. The only signs of life were roaming dogs. Finally we found a landmark noted on our bit of paper and breathed a sigh of relief; we were on the right track. The kids started muttering about this being one of Mum's specials where we end up in the middle of nowhere halfway up a mountain. As we drove along the valley floor, surrounded by olive trees on both sides, I noticed the lights of a small village in the distance, halfway up a mountain. *Oh Lord, please don't let that be our village.* Geoffrey also noticed it and groaned.

'I bet you've got us up there. It'd better be a proper road and not a bloody dirt track.'

'Of course it will be a proper road. I research these places thoroughly,' I retorted.

Finally we reached the end of the valley and surprise, surprise, we started to climb up a steep, switchback, dirt road with no lights or sign of life.

'Oh, this just smacks of Lake Como all over again, doesn't it?' moaned Geoffrey, referring to that previous changeover day that none of us would ever forget when we'd found ourselves frantically reversing out of the Swiss border post. The car fell silent again apart from the wipers.

'Why can't you ever find us somewhere normal to stay?' muttered one of the kids. 'Haven't you heard of hotels?'

The dirt road consisted of a reddish-coloured clay soil that was now becoming a mud road in the rain with the ruts disguised by the water. We bounced along, swerving to avoid rocks.

'Is this an actual road?' asked Don.

'Was that a fox?' I wondered, glimpsing a decidedly fox-like creature dash over the bank.

We came to a sudden halt when the road narrowed to one muddy lane and headed between two narrow, stone farm buildings.

'I don't believe it,' fumed Geoffrey. 'It's someone's rotten driveway.'

He stopped the car and we all sat there staring ahead in glum silence. Yep, it looked like we'd arrived at someone's farm. As I'd got us into this, I pulled out the cell phone to ring the houseowner, hoping they spoke some English. Jan meanwhile decided that her parents were utterly inept and took matters into her own hands. She took the torch and hopped out, walking forward into the rain and dark to see what was beyond the two stone buildings in front of us. She disappeared and I spoke to Sofia, the homeowner, who said her husband was searching for us. Jan reappeared from between the stone buildings and beckoned for us to follow. She'd found Dimitris.

We inched our way through the narrow gap with our mirrors wound in and bumped our way along a narrow, rough road between a handful of village houses, following Dimitris's car until he waved us into a parking space. They'd very kindly prepared for us a huge, traditional Greek meal of vine-wrapped stuffed tomatoes and opened a bottle of red wine. After they'd given us the instructions for the house, they set off back down the mountain to the town of Argos where they lived. The kids went off to explore the place while Geoffrey and I sat in the garden under a large umbrella with a very welcome drink in hand. We sat outside because there didn't appear to be a lot of furniture in the house.

Don and Jan returned and announced, 'Jeez, Mum, this place is for nudists.'

I just about choked on my wine and told them not to be ridiculous. But after I'd had a look around, it did seem to be a bit of a naturist retreat and I was forced to erect (excuse the choice of word) a screen to block off the shower which was open to view. Apart from this, rather than couches there were scatter cushions for lounging around on the floor, futon beds (very suspicious at the best of times) and a record player with a cache of old vinyl records, all clearly aimed at nude romps on the floor. With my dodgy foot and our combined creaky joints and bad backs, there was no way Geoffrey and I were going to be getting anywhere near floor level never mind romping on cushions.

I woke up next morning and went to leap out of bed but couldn't get up. The stupid futon was so low I couldn't make it to my feet. After rocking back and forth a few times to gain the momentum necessary to launch myself off it, I looked out of the window to see we were indeed high up a mountain, and yes, it was a goat track complete with goats wandering around with bells ringing and the sound of a donkey going hee-haw. It really was a stunning view. Parched, golden ground dotted in olive trees stretched out with a backdrop of layer upon layer of hills folding one behind the other in a blue haze as the sun rose. And there was Don out there, already poking around the garden with the wooden, curved walking stick that Sofia and Dimitris left us for scaring off any snakes or scorpions. They asked us to leave the garden gate shut to keep the foxes out. Don was very keen on finding any of the above.

GYPSIES AND FIRE

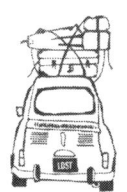

What immediately struck us about the Peloponnese was the evidence of the growing cash crisis, the poor condition of the roads, the wandering, starving dogs and the fact that someone had taken the time and trouble to go around even the most remote areas and spray-paint over the English translation on all road signs. All this hinted at the troubled financial and political times facing the people in this region.

On the second day, we returned to our house to find Greek Roma, or gypsies, camped 50 metres away in the small public space that served as a village square. It looked far more interesting than before and was now full of life with copperware on display and a fully working, open-air kitchen assembled with a pot bubbling away over a fire. The people were physically quite different to the locals, with much darker skin and sharper, more pointed features. They stared at us as we passed. We must have looked pretty alien to them too. Dimitris called them tinkers and told us the copperware on display was to advertise that they would clean and repair any you took to them in exchange for money or goods. He warned us to lock our doors. We didn't know if this was prejudice or experience talking.

As we knew nothing about them, we erred on the side of caution, deciding we weren't comfortable leaving the kids upstairs in separate accommodation as it wasn't linked to the house internally. We agreed that Geoffrey would sleep upstairs with Don, and Jan would sleep downstairs in the house with me. The kids discovered a huge projector screen upstairs that they insisted was used to play porn while the nudists romped on the cushions. We headed up to watch a DVD; no, not porn, just *Mrs Brown*. It was kind of hard to get comfy without furniture to sit on but we did our best.

With the lights out, we were watching *Mrs Brown* when smoke started to come in the open windows. Gypsy campfires, we presumed. The smoke increased and we got up to shut the windows. The screen got hazy with smoke hanging in the air so Geoffrey and I went to investigate. As we stepped outside, we were met by a smoke-filled garden and immediately started coughing. Geoffrey walked down the road with a torch to see if the smoke was coming from the gypsy camp; no, it wasn't. I checked inside and investigated all the electrical appliances; nothing obvious but downstairs was full of smoke as well. Down the road it was clear and up the road it was clear. It just seemed to be our place. We checked the outside lights, wondering if there was an electrical fire in one of the wires; still nothing. Geoffrey picked up his cell phone to ring Dimitris just as I spotted a fresh wall of smoke billowing down from the house behind and above us. They were having a burn-off. Mystery solved but highly irritating as we couldn't sit in the garden and our house was full of smoke.

The next night all this was forgotten and we headed out to the garden with a glass of wine. Then we heard a crackle and the fire was away again, with smoke billowing down onto us. We were forced to race indoors and shut the house up. It was so disappointing not to be able to enjoy the evening in the garden or even have a window open for air. I emailed Dimitris to let him know, emphasising that I realised it wasn't his fault but if he knew the neighbour, perhaps he could give them a call as maybe they didn't realise there were guests in residence. I was concerned that this was going to go on for the rest of the week.

I had a shower and we all got ready for an early night. I checked my email before heading to bed at 9:30 p.m. There was an email from Dimitris sent 30 minutes before saying this was unacceptable and that he was on his way to the house to rectify the problem.

'Oh shit,' I shouted. 'Dimitris is coming.'

'Oh no, I'm in my pyjamas,' groaned Jan.

'Me too. Oh God, look at all the mess.'

We scarpered upstairs and left Geoffrey to deal with things. I felt guilty and wondered how the neighbour would take it. It was such a tiny hamlet and we would now be as popular as bubonic plague. No one likes a moaning tourist who goes to a rural area then complains about the smells or noise.

We hid upstairs and a few minutes later saw the headlights of a car climbing the mountain. It came to a halt outside our house. Dimitris came in, spoke to Geoffrey then left. We heard the car roar up the road and stop above us. We stood with the door ajar, eavesdropping. After a minute or two, we heard Dimitris's voice talking in Greek to our neighbour. According to Geoffrey, the neighbours were new and Dimitris hadn't met them till now. A man's voice replied. The discussion got louder, followed by much shouting and rapid Greek. The yelling echoed loudly around the tiny hamlet.

What have I done? I cringed in the doorway, expecting a punch to be thrown. Then it all went quiet and voices returned to a normal level. Dimitris went inside with the man and we heard glasses clinking. He was in there for ages before returning to tell us that it was all sorted; the fire wouldn't be lit again. The neighbour could be heard above us, crashing around in the undergrowth, then water was poured on the fire. As Dimitris left we noticed the gypsies standing watching the drama. *Oh God, we'll probably be robbed and murdered in the night if Dimitris's opinions are to be believed.* I needed a huge wine.

Sometime in the night, I was woken suddenly by someone hovering over me. No, it wasn't the gypsies. It was Jan shouting in the darkness.

'Don't move. There's a spider above your head.'

As I have a spider phobia, I wasn't about to hang around and wait for it to land on me. I was out of there in a flash, futon or no futon.

Heart pumping, I leapt screaming from the bed. Then it dawned on me. It was dark. How the hell did Jan know there was a spider there?

'You're having that flipping bug dream again,' I shouted at her.

She insisted on checking the bed thoroughly before we climbed back in. Jan was asleep again in an instant. I however wasn't. I was wide awake. Gypsies or no gypsies, I was voting Jan out of the house next day.

PIRATE ISLAND

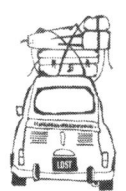

We'd just spent an unpleasant eleven hours in a car with only a two-hour break to take a day trip to Monemvasia, or Pirate Island as we called it. It's located on an island linked to the mainland by a causeway. This Byzantine fortress has withstood Arab and Norman invasion as well as regular raids by pirates for many centuries. It's surrounded by thick walls and has a labyrinth of tunnels running underneath it. I pictured Johnny Depp-type pirates roaming around and barrels of rum being rolled down into the tunnels. We simply had to go there.

After he'd studied the map before we set off, Geoffrey decided to stick to the main roads, even though it meant going quite a bit out of our way to get there. On paper it was 180 kilometres and we thought it'd take about three hours so left early; it took five. As per usual we got lost, finding ourselves in a maze of olive groves, going round and round and round. Marjorie was no help at all; the deranged madam commanded us to 'go left' at every intersection. I'm sure she was doing it deliberately just to wind his lordship up. It doesn't take a genius to work out that you end up going in a big circle if you keep turning left. Hence one hour was spent lost in the olives with no discernible difference in the landscape or a single signpost. The area was flat, with no high ground to try and see where the hell we were, so we just went up and down between rows of olives. Every road looked identical to the last: a carpet of parched, golden grass topped with silvery-leafed olive trees dripping in black olives. It was like someone with a very sick sense of humour had dumped us in an olive-tree maze with no way out.

Geoffrey just about had steam coming out his ears by this point and was going berserk, vehemently cursing about where he would like to shove their olive trees and why couldn't they chainsaw the wretched things down and use the wood to make some street signs. I noticed the kids grinning in the back seat. Their dad's outburst was the only interesting thing to happen in the last hour. At one point we sighted our destination off the coast. We felt a surge of excitement; yes, we were close. But the olives swallowed us up for another hour until we finally saw the sea again.

We had no idea where we were but at least we'd found the sea so it wouldn't be far. I demanded that Geoffrey pull over in a village so that I could do what women do best—ask for directions. I found a gorgeous, tanned Greek god and pointed to Monemvasia on the map and asked him to point out where we were now. Imagine my face when he said in a surprised voice, 'Madam, you are on the wrong side of the peninsula completely,' and pointed to our current location.

'Are you serious? I don't believe it,' I shrieked.

The Greek god kindly drew directions on my map and asked where we were from. He laughed when I said New Zealand. 'Good at rugby; not so good at navigating.' He chuckled as he wandered off.

Finally we arrived and it was truly amazing: the most captivating turquoise sea surrounding the straw-coloured island, with the village sitting snugly up against one side of the island. We accessed the fortified town through a solid stone archway that led into a short tunnel. As we emerged through the other side, it was like stepping back in time into a labyrinth of narrow, winding, cobbled lanes lined with bougainvillea and tightly packed, medieval houses. Sadly our pressing needs overshadowed the beauty as we sought out toilets and food. The doorways fascinated me with their ancient studwork, elaborate door knockers, peeling paint and giant keyholes. Arched porticos crossed the alleys between houses, hinting at days gone by when the residents needed to hide or escape.

We found a little restaurant sign and followed the lane up behind the stone building then up two flights of steep, ancient stone steps. We arrived at a rather unassuming-looking little door and were led out to a balcony high above the Aegean Sea. It was blissful; we could see for miles while we dined on beautiful food: delicate ravioli stuffed with salmon in a creamy dill sauce for Jan and me while Geoffrey and Don had spaghetti arrabbiata made with garlic, tomatoes and spicy red chilli peppers in olive oil.

Suitably replenished we set off to explore. The architecture was more 'Morocco meets Turkey' than Greek and the whole place was stunning. We didn't run into Johnny Depp but found the cannons poised pointing out to sea ready to fire at any approaching pirate ships. It was boiling hot so after another cold drink and an ice cream, it was time to face the long drive back. It was now 3:30 p.m. and I hoped to be home before dark.

After I'd studied the map, I made the stupid decision that we should return via the Eurotas Valley to the coast then follow the coastal road back to Nafplio and Argos. It seemed simple on paper but what the map didn't accurately convey was that the inconspicuous little squiggle was the greatest mountain range in the Peloponnese, extending right along the eastern edge of the peninsula inland from the Argolic Gulf.

Upon entering the Eurotas Valley, it appeared we'd been transported to the Grand Canyon, with towering, scarred, reddish limestone cliffs looming above a narrow river gorge. It wasn't too bad at the bottom but what goes down must come up and up and up, 1,100 metres into Mount Parnonas with a sheer drop on my side and light fading. We then stayed at that height for approximately two hours with absolutely no signs of civilisation. Winding our way along a cliff edge on a narrow rough road 1,100 metres high with no barrier wasn't my idea of a good time.

Everybody was quiet. Geoffrey couldn't even swear; he had to concentrate on staying on the road. If it hadn't been so terrifying, it would've been stunning. None of us had ever imagined seeing scenery like this on the Peloponnese but there was certainly nowhere to pull over and take a photo. We didn't see another car at all. I'm sure there was a reason for that but it made it all the more eerie. With the sun going down, the light played along the coloured layers of rock on the opposite cliff to us, lighting them up in a glow of pink, mauve and blue. We were above the tree line but below us were forests of black pine and fir. I later found out that this area was home to one of the last remaining populations of jackals. I couldn't help thinking that no one else in the world knew where we were right then and that if we went over the cliff, we would probably never be found.

The only life we saw was abandoned dogs plodding sadly along the edge of the road, skin and bone. They would stop when they heard our car and stand still, staring at us with big, sad, wide eyes as we drove by; it was heartbreaking, a sad testament to a country in financial crisis. The people didn't have the money to fix their roads never mind take care of dogs. If I could have, I would've gathered them all up, but what would I do with them? There was nowhere to take them. I shed a few silent tears behind my sunglasses. I also snivelled away to myself because I didn't think we were ever going to get off this godforsaken mountain and it had been a rotten road trip, even by our standards. To be fair, most of our family day trips involved being lost for a substantial amount of time but this one was off the flipping scale.

Right in the middle of the canyon, we drove beneath the 16th-century Elonis Monastery set into the sheer rock above us. I couldn't believe that anyone would build up there. It was just staggering; well, staggeringly stupid in my opinion. But I accept that if an enemy is trying to eradicate your religion, it pays to be in an inaccessible location. So I gave them ten points for that one.

Nearly three hours later we finally emerged from the mountain gorge to the coast where we spent a further hour winding along the cliffs above the ocean. It was now dark; there were a few abandoned fishing and holiday villages interspersed along the route. At one point our headlights picked up a dark shape in the middle of the road. We slowed down and stopped; a large tortoise was crossing the road. We all stared at it as we don't have tortoises in New Zealand. There wasn't enough room on the narrow road to go around it safely without risking going over the cliff.

When I say the tortoise was crossing the road, it had actually stopped. We waited. It sat. We waited. It sat some more. Geoffrey started huffing and puffing.

'You'll have to move it,' I said.

'Do tortoises bite?' Geoffrey asked Don.

'How should I know?'

'Well you're our Gerald Durrell.'

Geoffrey got out and approached the tortoise nervously. He made shooing noises and flapped his arms about, keeping a wary distance. We all laughed hysterically.

'What do tortoises eat?' I asked Don.

'Why does everyone keep asking me about tortoises?'

'Well you're good at reptile-type things: snakes, salamanders, crocodiles,' I said. 'Go and help your father; try luring it with food; take some of those biscuits.'

We all got out and stood staring at the tortoise in the darkness. Don waved a biscuit in front of its head.

'Do they have a nose?' asked Jan.

'Unbelievable,' muttered Geoffrey and stomped back to the car.

'Maybe we could just shove it,' I suggested.

'They have long necks,' Don informed us. 'It might whip its head around and bite us.'

'I've gone right off tortoises,' I replied and nudged it from behind with my shoe. It looked around at me with its beady eyes. I gave it another nudge and it took a step forward. Yes, a few more helpful, gentle shoves and it carried on over the road, keen to escape the morons.

We managed to see a lot of the Peloponnese in one day. It was stunning but we would prefer to have seen less of it. We finally made it home at 9:30 p.m., thirteen hours after setting off. We all had motion sickness and felt like we were still swaying hours afterwards. No amount of wine could manage to eradicate that drive from my memory. Don headed off to Google tortoises; Geoffrey and I headed to the garden with a drink and Jan went to Facebook her friends about the day's adventures.

BLIND NINJAS INVADE COLLIOURE AND WHAT NOT TO DO AT A CHIC MEDITERRANEAN BEACH

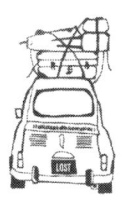

After we left Greece, we flew to Toulouse in France and drove to Carennac in the Dordogne area for a week before heading south to Collioure for the next leg of our trip. We'd said a delighted farewell to maddening Marjorie and replaced her with the equally ludicrous La La. We'd just come in from a swim in the Mediterranean, right in front of our apartment. We were staying in a gated community with our own beach directly below us, probably 25 metres from our door. As soon as we arrived the day before, we headed into the sea. The rest of the family all swam and I made a spectacle of myself. I'll explain shortly.

Changeover day as we'd left Carennac had gone reasonably smoothly. We shouldn't really have got lost at all from there, given that we'd been to Collioure before. It's a beautiful little French fishing village on the southwest Mediterranean coast only about twenty kilometres from the Spanish border. Officially it's in the Pyrenees department but is more Catalan than French. As per usual we took a wrong turn and ended up in the next town along, Port-Vendres. It should have been a simple matter of turning around and going back but we couldn't find our way out. I know you must be thinking by now that we're quite stupid but I promise you that we aren't so let's just call us navigationally challenged. Somehow we found ourselves juddering our way along a wooden wharf, where a ship was being loaded, trying to avoid piles of nets and floats.

I tried talking in a calm, soothing, low tone of voice to Geoffrey, as though he was a cat, hoping he wouldn't self-combust. I decided it was time to give La La the satnav a chance to redeem herself. I switched her on and set her to our destination. And blow me down, that irksome little creature took control of the situation and calmly guided Geoffrey off the wharf and out of Port-Vendres back to Collioure. Contrary little madam. Why couldn't she be like that all the time? We arrived at our apartment without Geoffrey having a tanty which was quite annoying as I had a $10 bet with Jan that he would have one before we arrived.

We dumped the bags and the family all headed straight into the water.

I waded out, intending to have a paddle, then stopped dead. The sea floor dropped away steeply and I was left balanced precariously on the edge of a precipice with my feet sinking deeply and unevenly into the fine, soft shingle. I was stuck. Not a problem if you can swim, but I can't, not one stroke. My wonderful family had swum off into the bay and abandoned me. I looked behind me at the audience of sun-baking, athletic, brown bodies. What to do? I knew with my complete lack of balance and coordination the slightest movement was going to see me topple over into the abyss. So I chose to appear nonchalant, like I was deliberately standing like a statue. To achieve the casual look and not seem like a twit that was stuck, I whistled, didn't I, and gazed around like I was admiring the view.

One of the athletic ones in his tight budgie smugglers came in for a swim. I smiled and casually flicked my hands in the water as if, yes, I was just warming up. The athletic Mr Swanky-Pants dived off the precipice and swam off. I maintained my nonchalant look as best I could while feeling like a complete noddy, realising that I must appear quite odd to all the eyes behind me, having been rooted to the spot for a good 30 minutes. I silently seethed at Geoffrey frolicking out in the bay until he finally came close enough for me to hiss, 'I'm stuck.'

'What?' asked the gormless twit.

'I'm stuck. Get me out,' I hissed louder.

Geoffrey came over, grabbed my hands and yanked me out like he was pulling a giant turnip from the ground. Finally, with a bit of a pop, I was released and he helped me hobble back to shore where I staggered from the water, kept my head down and scuttled back to the apartment. *You wait*, I thought. *I'll be back*.

Next morning we went into Collioure for a wander and a coffee, did some grocery shopping and had lunch on our balcony followed by a sea-air-induced siesta. Then at 3-ish, everyone started coming out of their apartments and setting up at the beach. This time I was prepared as thankfully Geoffrey didn't cark it[1] trying to blow up my new floatee. Earlier in the morning, we'd found a bunch of beach equipment stuffed behind the washing machine. Among it all was the biggest floatee ring I'd ever seen. I was back. Loud and proud I marched down to that beach in front of all the gorgeous people, an enormous, striped floatee around my middle, and flopped my way out to the precipice. Tanned heads adorned with designer sunglasses all turned in my direction. With a leap and a splash reminiscent of a whale breaching, I was off.

'Look at me,' I shouted to Don. 'I'm floating.'

I was able to bob out over the reef where I could see all the cool-looking fish below me. At that moment I wasn't fat. I was free, buoyant and floating in the deliciously cool, super-clear water; it felt magnificent. Suddenly the rising breeze caught my bobbing flotation device and I found myself heading out to sea. Overcome with panic I started screaming as I saw the news headlines flash before me: Fat Lady in Giant Floatee Swept out to Sea. An image of a shark came to mind. Suddenly something grabbed my foot. I was about to yell till I realised Don was yanking me back to shore. 'Oh thank God. I thought you were a shark,' I said.

'Don't be stupid,' he replied.

My landing back on shore wasn't such a graceful, floaty thing, more of a lurch, squelch, lurch, squelch as I wobbled my way up the sloping mass of painful, sucking, horrible stones with my blubbery bits wobbling. I hate people who seem to glide in and out effortlessly. How do they even do that?

After this incident the family ensured they all stayed on the seaward side of me and took it in turns to tow Mother back in when the breeze and current drifted her out again.

It was now Tuesday and what an interesting day we'd had. First stop was the bakery to get our lunch supplies. I'd made sure we held onto the raspberry tart correctly as the baker had got upset with my tart-handling skills the previous day. Only in France could a baker get away with chasing a customer down the street to snatch back his tarts with much tutting and overly dramatic shaking of his head. After rearranging them he'd passed them carefully to a more trustworthy sort, in this case Don the brown-noser. Such a suck-up, Don; a bit of secondary school French and suddenly he could do no wrong. The French are so passionate about their food, bless them, and to see me foolishly risking a broken tart was obviously very distressing. Sacrebleu!

Then we did some mime work at the tourist office. France was the only place we'd found staff in a tourist office that didn't speak English or, according to Geoffrey, pretended they didn't. It was rather difficult to communicate using our Frenglish so in the end we gave up, nodded and smiled, saying *oui, oui* to everything the woman said. We hadn't a clue what was happening but there you go. We would find out on the day. We hoped the end result was that we were going on a bus to Villefranche-de-Conflent on the Thursday, leaving at 6:30 a.m. to catch the world-renowned, little yellow tourist train up into the Pyrenees Mountains.

We were just approaching the small bridge that led up to the Château Royal in Collioure when a group of blind ninjas first appeared. Now just to explain—they weren't really blind ninjas but looked just like Buster Brady's blind ninjas from *Mrs Brown's Boys D'Movie*, all in black, walking in a row. (In case you're not familiar with the movie, Buster, an infamous troublemaker, recruits a troop of blind, trainee ninjas and these men in Collioure were similar, all dressed in black and with blackened, camouflaged faces.)

The sight of all these figures in tight, black wetsuit bottoms and camouflage tops with guns slung over their broad shoulders, emerging from a drainage ditch that led out to sea, soaking wet and dragging kayaks behind them, was enough to stop me in my tracks. For one thing it was so incongruous. We were in a little village teeming with tourists and holidaymakers; what the hell were these gorgeous, camouflaged creatures doing emerging out of a drain? Oh, and that was the other thing that stopped me in my tracks and had my camera clicking away furiously—they were HOT.

I was jolted back to reality by the impatient voices of my children. I told them the castle could wait; this was better and I wasn't budging. I sent them to get gelato as I was focused on taking in the sights. The blind ninjas carried their kayaks, packs and guns under the bridge and through the castle's moat. Excellent. I could stand on the bridge and watch as they hosed the seawater off themselves and stacked their kayaks while my camera clicked away. Jan hissed at me to stop being such a perv and pointed out that I was acting like a cougar. I looked around me. Every other able-bodied female in the vicinity was lined up along the bridge railing with me, all eyes focused on ogling the mysterious men in black. Once the men finished sorting their gear, they headed through an opening below the château to shower.

Who were these camouflaged, face-painted ninjas? Where did they come from? Why were they there? I eventually found a sign which explained that this was a French commando training centre and learnt that the trainees were subjected to mental stress and physical fatigue while trying to find the strength to accomplish their military tasks. The centre trains men and women in the armed services to survive in war zones. The trainee commandos have to endure limited food and sleep while being put through a succession of intense day- and night-time activities. *How cool is that?* I thought. *Absolutely not what I expected to find in this little seaside village.* Anyway, enough of that. The commandos were now somewhere beneath the castle. I hollered at the others that I was now very eager to go and explore it, or what was currently inside it; they had to be in there somewhere.

Sadly I didn't find the ninjas but by the time we reached the top of the castle and were looking over the turrets, we spotted two small Navy ships docking down below with successions of blind ninjas streaming into the bowels of the castle. Meanwhile in the other direction in the little bay to our right, a small crowd had formed. Yet more were all geared up with heavy loads. Their chief commando instructed them on the shore then sent them all into the water where they were forced to stay afloat treading water while carrying heavy loads or a body-shaped dummy. I hustled and frogmarched the family out of the château, stopping just long enough to grab another gelato, then hotfooted it around the castle wall to sit and watch the progress. Holidaymakers lined the wall, licking gelato and watching the figures in black suffering; kind of voyeuristic and sadistic at the same time. This was way better than watching children frolic at the water's edge.

The blind ninjas remained a constant presence over the week, zipping around the coast in their Zodiacs or Navy vessels or diving in groups. Our little bay was used for diving whenever it was too rough offshore. The Navy vessels also came in close to shore, anchoring next to the swimmers. I was in the perfect spot to sit myself down on the balcony with a cuppa or a glass of wine, binoculars superglued to my eyeballs while I enjoyed the ninja action. We became accustomed to their sudden appearance sprinting in single file through the town, blackened faces, camouflage gear and loaded down with heavy packs. They would dash through the throngs of startled tourists, looking so blatantly out of place.

When I told my mother in New Zealand about them over the phone, she was pretty excited and announced that they would be training to swim to Iraq. I just about fell off my chair laughing, trying to picture this in my mind.

'Do you even know where Iraq is?' I asked.

I put Geoffrey on the phone while I finished choking.

'It's in the middle of the desert,' I heard him say, sounding incredulous. 'They would have to swim about 3,000 kilometres,' he added, laughing. 'But to be fair, it does have one wee bit that borders water on the Persian Gulf.'

One night during the week we were fast asleep in our room overlooking the bay when a horrendous din suddenly woke us.

'Bloody Nora, what's that?' groaned Geoffrey.

The noise was coming from outside. I bolted for the deck.

'Oh my God, the blind ninjas are invading,' I shouted.

A mass of sinister black shapes in Zodiacs were moving in one long line at high speed into our bay with the scream of a hundred Zodiac engines buzzing. They had no lights; we could just see their outline in the light of the full moon.

'Well they can *sod off*,' groaned Geoffrey, pulling the pillow over his head. I headed out of the room. 'Where are you going?' he asked.

'To watch, of course,' I replied, grabbing the binoculars and heading onto the balcony. The ninjas zoomed ashore, decided there were no terrorists hidden in our tourist community and departed again. On other nights we saw them doing the same, only rather than a high-speed attack it would be the slow and stealthy approach without making a sound. Either method worked for me.

Later in the week, I found myself aboard another floating vessel; this one was taking us out to sea from Port-Vendres and along the coast. The open sea looked rather rough to me but Geoffrey assured me it wasn't and that there would be a gangplank. Of course there wasn't. Idiot. But the skipper and deckhand just pulled me on board. Personally I would've preferred to be manhandled by the blind ninjas; these two weren't up to standard.

The kids wanted to sit outside on the catamaran's bow and told me it was the calmest part of the boat. Indeed all was calm in the harbour: sun shining and a flat ocean. I hate the sea and I hate being on a boat, but hey, this was OK. I started to relax. We left behind the protection of the sea wall and entered open water. Far out, suddenly the horizon was gone and I was looking at the sky. My stomach stayed up in the air but the rest of me crashed down into the trough of the wave. My stomach rejoined me but not for long as we were looking at the sky again before lurching down. I clutched the sides of the seat with white knuckles; it was like a roller coaster. The kids thought it was great, especially the tortured look on my face.

I was trapped and had to wait ages for a gap between swells before lurching indoors and sitting myself next to a lifesaver ring and the flotation devices. We stopped in the shelter of a calm bay for the passengers to go down below water level to watch through the glass as the fish were fed. Everyone disappeared down below. The deckhand came and asked why I wasn't going too.

'Fish are only good fried and served with chips,' I said.

He backed away from me looking nervous and uncomfortable at finding himself in the presence of a nutter. No point scaring the man with my many phobias; easier just to let him think I hated fish. I sat alone on the boat, admiring the view and pondering how someone who hates boats kept finding herself on them so often and came to the conclusion that it was all Geoffrey's fault. Well, not really. I just try not to let my 'issues' interfere with everyone else's plans. My only request was that he found me boats with a gangplank; a task he'd failed miserably on so far. He should take a leaf out of Captain Hook's book; *he* had no trouble finding planks!

---

1. Die.

COUCHES AND COACHES

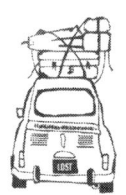

That night we decided to watch a bit of *Miranda* on DVD so Geoffrey tried to open the sofa bed in the living room so we could sprawl out on it. No response. He pulled again—nothing —then got Jan and I on one end and himself on the other. He decided we were going to force it to open. We succeeded, with a horrible noise of metal grinding and twisting. We froze; that didn't sound good.

Miranda was forgotten. Geoffrey had a tanty as we frantically tried to put the sofa back together. To our horror it no longer bent.

'Shit, you've broken it,' we said accusingly to Geoffrey.

He had a look of fear in his eyes as he calculated how much we would have to pay the landlord for a replacement bed.

'Bugger it,' he said and announced that he would fix it himself. He dispatched me to study my holiday French book for useful phrases we would need such as 'my husband has broken the bed; I need a wrench and a mallet'. Strangely enough the phrase book didn't include any useful hardware-shop words. I would imagine this is because most vacationers aren't as accident prone as us. They're probably not such skinflints either and would just pay the owner for the repair or replacement, but not Geoffrey. He ordered Jan to Google our nearest hardware store.

The next morning, as the other members of our gated community were setting up down at the beach, we set off on a mission, clutching the instructions for finding the store. All was quiet in the car; we knew better than to aggravate Geoffrey when he was on a knife's edge. The store looked rather like our typical Mitre 10 back in New Zealand. Of course each aisle's contents were written in French so we just cruised them till we found what we needed. The lady on the checkout was clearly not used to serving idiotic holidaymakers and insisted on talking to us in rapid French. We just stood there, grinning and mute. My knowledge of French only extended to ordering gelato and wine, not bed-fixing tools. We shrugged in that typically French way and left.

Back at the apartment, we shut all doors and windows while the clandestine bed repair got underway. We didn't want any nosy neighbours to report either the noise or the suspicious activity. Geoffrey used the wooden, baguette-chopping board in the absence of a work bench and set to with the mallet. Oh my God; the racket of metal being pounded with a wooden hammer ricocheted around the small and completely tiled space. Sunbathers' heads turned to look up. The kids and I crouched away from the windows so that nobody could see us and prayed Geoffrey would be quick before the caretaker came pounding on our door to kick us out. Operation mallet over, Geoffrey called for Jan and me to help force the bed back into a closed position. Finally we managed to shut the darned thing and no one dared sit on it for the rest of the week.

ONE WAY

We had an early start next day with our bus trip to Villefranche-de-Conflent and then the train up into the mountains to the highest train station in France. The little yellow train of the Pyrenees is one of the great railway journeys of the world. Opened in 1909 it travels through dramatic scenery from 427 metres to an altitude of 1,592 metres. We were looking forward to this, having been unable to get tickets on our last trip.

'Now what's going on?' was a question we asked a lot that day. It confirmed for us that coach trips suck and were definitely not for us. At 6:20 a.m. the bus arrived at Collioure virtually empty. But predictably some people had to push in front of others; the rudest were two ladies who barged past everyone, including the elderly and a disabled gentleman. I nicknamed them the Jack Russells because of the way they were practically nipping at everyone's heels.

The bus stopped at a few other points to collect the rest of the passengers and then the commentary started up...all in French. Which was fine; we were, after all, in France. It was interspersed with a bit of German and Spanish for the other passengers, but no English. We didn't mind missing out on the commentary and had no expectations but just a few words to let us know why we were stopping, for how long, what we were supposed to be looking at and when to be back at the bus might have been useful.

Hence our repeated use of *'now* what's going on?' as we blindly followed others around the place all day, trying to guess what was happening. When it was time to get on the train, the Jack Russells again sprang from nowhere, leapt in front of everyone already waiting to board and shoved their way on. Once happily seated and full of excitement, we were off. Three stops later and before we'd even risen into the high Pyrenees, we were ordered off.

Apparently we were on the skinflint tour where rather than paying the cost of the complete train journey, they picked us all up in the bus three stops after setting off. Why pay extra when they could drive us around on their bus more cheaply, stopping to show us rubbish instead of letting us enjoy a spectacular train journey high into the Pyrenees?

This is how it went: the bus would stop; the driver would tell everyone else in their language what was happening and they would all get off. Where were they going, we wondered? At one point the bus stopped so we could photograph what can only be described as a monstrosity of an ugly square building covered in tin foil.

'What the hell is that?' asked Geoffrey.

In the end I couldn't be bothered and just stayed on the bus sulking. Each time Geoffrey got back on, I asked, 'What was it?'

'No idea,' he would reply. We wished we were still on the train taking the journey we thought we'd signed up for. We'd asked the driver if he could speak any English but got a very firm and unapologetic, *'Non.'*

The bus parked in a deserted ski village, and I mean deserted, as in ghost town; there were no people, no cars, nothing open and nothing to do. What better place for a skinflint tours' lunch stop? The driver said a few words in French, German and Spanish so that everyone would know what was happening (except us) then they got off. We picked up on a couple of words and numbers, recognising bon appetit, so guessed we were stopping here in no man's land for lunch. Were we meant to find lunch in this seemingly deserted ghost town? The other passengers all followed the driver so we tagged along behind. He led everyone into a restaurant where there appeared to be a Spanish buffet. The tables were laid with plates upon which were tiny slithers of melon with ham on top so we sat down. We presumed it was included in the cost. We were beyond petulant by now.

Low and behold, who was left to sit with us? The Jack Russells! So being a bit naughty and knowing they probably didn't speak much English, I said in a loud voice, 'Sooooo, did you see those Jack Russells pushing their way through the crowd?'

Jan and Don got into it and Jan replied, 'Yes, they seemed a bit inbred.'

'I think they were mongrels,' said Don.

'They weren't very well trained, were they?' I asked.

'They need to go back to obedience training,' added Jan.

''Bout time they had a good bath,' sniggered Don.

And so it went on. Poor Geoffrey was most confused and kept asking, 'What Jack Russells? I didn't see any?'

Oh dear, clueless as per usual.

Anyway I digress. Back to lunch. The table was laden with red wine, rosé, sangria, champagne then spirits with coffee. I found this rather odd. Had the wrong bus trip turned up for lunch? Were they expecting a party bus full of Contiki-type youth? Most of the passengers on our coach were well into their twilight years. We presumed it was all free and included in the trip. The maître d' greeted the group and appeared to be explaining a bit about where we were. We had no idea where the hell we were. We thought we were in France but the Spanish food, sangria and Spanish costumes were telling us otherwise. We hadn't seen any border crossing. We were most confused and trapped in a maddening game of mime.

After the starter the Spanish maître d' brought out a card game and explained to everyone in French, German and Spanish how to play. We watched the gestures, trying to pick up on nonverbal clues. There was laughter and applause. The maître d' shuffled the cards dramatically and handed them out. He then pulled a couple of cards from the deck. I lost interest and tried the sangria. Geoffrey nudged me. I turned and had to do a double take. Two of the pensioners were up the front, playing a drinking game. The Spaniards were pouring some sort of alcohol out of a jug and down a tube; the players had to stand under it and catch the drink in their mouths. Don and Jan sat, eyes bulging, transfixed by this unusual spectacle. Were these pensioners the winners or losers of the card game, I wondered.

I was dumbfounded. What sort of people pour grog down pensioners' throats? Not that they seemed to be complaining. Perhaps all the cheap grog was to put the passengers in a happy mood so they would forget what a lousy day they'd had, forget that they didn't actually do the train journey but that they'd travelled for miles to see a box covered in tin foil then had to sit and have a rubbish lunch at a table with two Jack Russells.

We were served a plate of really awful paella, so oversalted it was inedible, followed by a sliver of ice cream.

'Just as well we're not paying for this shit,' said Geoffrey.

There was a round of applause about something and the Spanish guy started walking around collecting money. I watched closely and saw the Jack Russells were each counting out the same amount—€17. I nudged Geoffrey. He groaned loudly. We now had to pay for the awful food and a ton of booze we didn't drink. Combined with the quarter of a train trip and a guide who refused to speak English, skinflint tours were on a roll.

'Drink that sangria,' commanded Geoffrey. 'If I'm paying for it, they aren't getting it back.'

That's the last time I do a bus tour. I would rather be permanently lost in La La land than ever set foot on a bus again.

LA LA STRIKES AGAIN AND THE DANGEROUS CREATURES OF PROVENCE

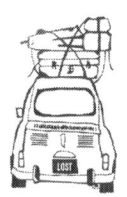

We'd moved on to Bonnieux, Provence, for a three-day stop-off on our way to Italy. It's in the Luberon Valley, famed for Peter Mayle's setting of his book *A Year in Provence*. We were staying at Le Gendarmerie, a former police station that had been converted into beautiful apartments overlooking a central pool. Most importantly it had parking, washing machine, air con and Wi-Fi. Better still, it was set in a beautiful hilltop village of honey-coloured stone, with a bakery and grocer's two minutes' stroll from the door as well as a selection of cafés and restaurants nearby. We were repeat visitors, this being our third time at Le Gendarmerie.

We headed to Avignon, with Geoffrey programming La La not just for Avignon but also its Palace of the Popes. This was a big mistake. But first, as we approached the city, we came to a large intersection where a group of gypsies were working the area, washing car windows uninvited and aggressively demanding cash. A group of them approached our car and we shook our heads and said no. Undeterred they started cleaning the front windscreen. I glanced at Geoffrey and was perturbed by the familiar look on his face but was distracted by the sudden screams coming from outside the car. I looked around, taking in the sight of angry gypsies disentangling their fingers and gear from under the wiper blades which were now going at high speed.

'Geoffrey, I can't believe you just did that,' I shouted. 'You could've hurt them.'

'I know,' he said and off we drove with the light turning green in the nick of time.

'We'll probably have a curse on us now,' said one of the bright sparks in the back seat.

'Really? Well how will we be able to tell?' asked Geoffrey. 'Every day is already one long bum ache after another.'

We thought La La would lead us to the nearest car park to the palace but no, she proudly and obediently delivered us right to the door. I first became concerned when she demanded we enter the castle walls through an archway. From my check on TripAdvisor, I thought we needed to park outside the walls. However, Geoffrey was already turning in. We later discovered that traffic within the old city was for hotels, service vehicles and residents only. We bumped our way over the ancient and noisy, teeth-jarring cobbles through a maze of alarmingly narrow lanes in silence. Eventually we emerged into a vast square with La La proudly and triumphantly announcing that we'd reached our destination.

We stared up at the enormous castle looming before us. The only thing stopping us from reaching the palace's front door was the diners eating in the courtyard.

'You lobotomised twit,' said Geoffrey, slamming the steering wheel. The diners turned to look at the idiots trying to drive into the palace. Geoffrey headed on into the maze of cobbled lanes. La La screamed at him repeatedly to do a U-turn.

'Turn that thing off,' snapped Geoffrey. The kids sniggered in the back seat and imitated their father.

'I need a coffee,' whined Jan.

'This is the curse of the gypsies,' laughed Don.

After we'd left the car at a car park building outside the walls, we returned to the square on foot. Jan was fast heading into caffeine withdrawal and needed coffee quickly so we dashed into the nearest café. I bravely forged ahead with my very best travel French; the man looked quite surprised. *Must be impressed*, I thought to myself proudly. He prepared the coffees then ran next door into the ice cream parlour and came back with ice cream which he dutifully dolloped into our coffees. We all stared with raised eyebrows.

'Why the heck did he put ice cream in our coffee?' I whispered to the kids.

'Because you told him to,' replied Don smugly.

Oh, no wonder he looked surprised. My linguistic confidence shrivelled a bit more.

After our unusual coffee/ice cream duo, we entered the Palace of the Popes, the largest Gothic building of the Middle Ages which formed the seat of Western Christianity during the 14th century, housing six of the Avignon popes. The Gothic architectural style of the building was impressive with its creamy-toned stone façade and arches, pointed turrets and arrow slits overlooked by the battlements. After being suitably impressed, we wandered the old town and had a tasty lunch of magret de canard and duck confit with potato gratin and French beans at a café.

We returned home via the supermarket where we grabbed some cold drinks to cool off before setting off again towards our village of Bonnieux in the Luberon Valley. It was a pleasant 25 degrees. Don started whinging about his can of fizzy peach drink being disgusting. I told him to stop moaning and drink the damn thing. Ten minutes later he said, 'But, Mum, it tastes like Dad's beer.'

'What?' That got my attention. 'Pass it here.' I took a swig. 'Oh my God, Don's sitting in the back swigging a beer,' I announced. I was more than happy to swap drinks with him. We'd confused the French word for peach—*pêche*—with the word for a shandy—*panaché*. Oops.

When we got back, Jan headed off into the village to shop and we all leapt in the pool at Le Gendarmerie. Well, gingerly lowered ourselves as the water was polar cold. I found a giant inflatable dolphin that someone had left there and I pleaded with poor Geoffrey to blow it up for me. It was the sort of size that ordinarily would require a pump so he wasn't best pleased. The veins in his head popped out alarmingly and his face turned a lovely shade of crimson. But just think, finally I could venture down the deep end riding on my dolphin. Yes, I can hear you laughing, thank you very much, and yes, I know those things are for kids, but if you can't swim, you can't swim. I was looking forward to being liberated from the steps of the pool.

Once I was aboard my new-found dolphin friend and floating over the deep end, I discovered the reason it had been abandoned. It had a hole in it. I found this out when I was forced to frantically give it mouth to mouth as it tried to sink me by rolling onto its back as it slowly deflated.

'It's going into a death roll,' shouted Geoffrey, looking rather smug.

'It's not a crocodile,' I yelled back.

The dolphin wasn't the only dangerous creature at the pool. Don, with his talent for finding wildlife, spotted a black scorpion right beside it. In fact he nearly stepped on it. We all rushed over to examine the creature with great interest.

We also discovered that Provence is full of a terrifying breed of giant Asian hornet. They're not your typical wasp; the Asian hornet is the largest wasp in the world and stings its victims multiple times using a potent venom containing eight different chemicals. It had killed six people in France in the previous year alone. It grows to a terrifying seven and a half centimetres in length. This hideous torpedo of death was attracted to our peaceful outdoor French picnic on our deck, causing us to run screaming inside. From the safety of the other side of the French door, we were left watching the hornet sampling our food until we shoved Geoffrey out with a rolled-up magazine to dispatch it. Sadly its friends arrived and we were forced to allow Geoffrey back inside. The hornets enjoyed their picnic.

We decided to try a little rooftop restaurant in the village overlooking the valley below for our last night in Bonnieux. Once we entered we discovered that it was rather more upmarket than we'd anticipated. We were surrounded by quiet and poised couples trying to have romantic dinners. It was *very* quiet. I warned everyone to behave. Geoffrey ordered what he thought was a glass of rosé for us both but it turned out to be a carafe each. 'Well, I've paid for it, I'll drink it,' was his attitude. We were happily imbibing at our table on the edge of the terrace next to a beautiful window box of flowers. Suddenly another giant Asian hornet dive-bombed the wine. Our table erupted in terrified screams and frantic swatting with the menus and serviettes. This only served to anger the hornet who continued to dive-bomb his petrified prey until eventually Geoffrey trapped him in a glass where we left him angrily glaring at us. So there we were in the romantic setting: four Kiwis and our loudly buzzing pet, Harry the hornet, flapping furiously around the glass. We laughed helplessly. The more rosé we drank, the louder we became. By we, I mean Geoffrey.

But the ultra-humiliation came as we tried to leave the terrace. Geoffrey led the way and walked straight into a glass partition, glancing off it with a look of surprise. He then staggered along the length of the glass trying to get out while we, his supportive family, were doubled over laughing. Finally the maître d' took pity on us fools and released us by opening a very simple-looking sliding door. It was lucky we were leaving next morning.

Just to complete our study of Provençal wildlife, Don and I were hanging out of the bedroom shutters before bed, enjoying watching the bats flitting around below in the light of the street lamps. We simultaneously recoiled in horror as a bat swooped straight past our faces and into the bedroom. I screamed and ran out, slamming the door behind me, leaving Don shut in with the bat. He dived under the duvet and lay there with the covers over him.

'What's it doing?' I shouted to him.

'It's flying. What the heck do you think it's doing?' he yelled back.

I sent Geoffrey in with a towel to try and capture it but by the time he woke himself up fully from his booze-laden snooze, the bat had let itself out.

'Shit, it's pooped all over the pillow,' shouted Geoffrey.

Bonne nuit. Good night.

WE ARE NOT GOING TO VENICE

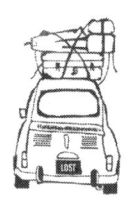

As we left Provence, we followed the autoroute high above the Mediterranean, snaking around the cliffs and viaducts above the pastel towns clinging to the rocks above the bright blue waters of the Italian Riviera. Levanto lies just over an hour south of Genoa between its more glitzy neighbours of Portofino and the Cinque Terre on the Ligurian coast. Our budget didn't allow us to stay there but Levanto made an ideal base for a few days to explore the coast.

I woke up in the night to the sound of a Boeing engine revving in the bathroom. I thought I must be hallucinating on the local red wine but there it was again, gathering force, ready for lift-off. Oh my God. I sat up and put the light on. No Geoffrey, so I went to investigate and found the Boeing with his head down the toilet. Yuck.

So we were having a home day at our holiday rental. I'd been checking details for Venice, our next stop. Geoffrey was totally against it in principle: full of pretentious prats, too pricey, too smelly, too crowded and most of all it was on his banned list of places he refuses to drive to. The others on that list are Rome and Paris, any big city really, and having read this book so far, you'll realise why as it doesn't take much imagination to predict the result of us driving into these places. Hence I didn't exactly tell Geoffrey we were going to Venice; I thought I would surprise him when it was too late for him to do anything about it. While he was in a weakened state seemed to be just the right opportunity to give him the news.

We could only afford three nights in Venice as it really was expensive. I know some of you will have the impression that we're rich and should've been able to afford to stay in Venice for as long as we liked but that couldn't be further from the truth. We're not well-heeled travellers at all; it's just that we put travel ahead of more practical things. My watch is a plastic one from a bargain shop and if you gave me a diamond, I would cash it in to go travelling. We have to borrow, scrimp and save for these experiences and appreciate every minute of them. Hence on these trips we mostly cooked for ourselves and took only a few meals out.

I'd tried to minimise Geoffrey's stress levels by pre-organising things to make life easier. I thought if I knew exactly how to get to Venice, where we were leaving the car, how and where to catch the water taxi then nothing could go wrong to tip him over the edge. Hence I'd spent countless hours on the internet before departure, researching. I'd booked and paid for our car to be parked in a secure garage at the end of the bridge over to Venice. I'd even done a satellite Google walk from the car park building to the water bus and taxi area. Never before had I been so prepared for a destination. I'd planned with military precision and secrecy.

I found a highly recommended hotel on TripAdvisor that had family apartments with kitchen and a washing machine. *Excellent. That will save money if we continue to eat in and it'll keep Geoffrey calm.* However, while checking the fine print, I discovered you had to pay €50 to unlock and use the oven in the kitchen and a further €15 to unlock the washing machine. So clearly the fact that I could buy a small car with what I was paying for three nights wasn't enough; they'd found another way of sucking cash out of me. Perhaps Geoffrey was right; maybe they were all pretentious prats. But Geoffrey mustn't find out, not a word.

I'd pre-booked tickets to Saint Mark's Basilica and the Doge's Palace to minimise the chances of Geoffrey having a tanty standing in a long queue. Despite the cost I was very excited to see Venice; it was one of those places I'd always dreamt of visiting but couldn't because it was on the banned list. Well, I'd unbanned it and Geoffrey would just have to deal with it.

I was so in love with Venice that I was too excited to sleep the night before we left, knowing we were going there. Geoffrey also had a wakeful night after I broke the news to him, but for different reasons. The atmosphere in the car as we drove into the outskirts of the city was intense. I was totally focused on not letting anything go wrong. All lanes led to the Ponte della Libertà over the Venetian Lagoon. It was like being in the spout of a funnel waiting to be spat out into the bowels of Venice. We were sandwiched between cars, buses and a train line, all heading to the same destination. Thank God I'd done a satellite Google search as when we were inevitably spat out of the funnel at the end of the line, I was able to find the parking garage easily amidst the spilling chaos and confusion of thousands of tourists pouring into one spot all at once. The noise and activity of everyone trying to park, drag suitcases to the canal or get on and off buses, boats and trains was bewildering.

Geoffrey was taking a 'you brought us here; it's your problem' stance. So when we found ourselves stuck in a long line of vehicles waiting to book into the garage, I was forced to sort things myself. I jumped out of the car and went to the head of the queue to wave my pre-paid voucher at the men doing the sorting. It was our VIP ticket to the front and we were waved in, bypassing all the cars sitting in the hot sun. The garage San Marco seemed to be very well run, with someone watching each level of the building at all times. This eased Geoffrey's concerns about leaving our main suitcases in the boot.

I then took charge and led the way to the waterfront where I'd planned to get a water taxi rather than the water bus direct to the hotel. This would've saved us from getting lost in Venice searching for our hotel. Yeah right, that must be someone else's book. Of course plans went astray slightly. The tide was at the wrong level for the water taxi to take us to the hotel so it was on to plan B. I tried to recall the information from TripAdvisor while appearing to know exactly what I was doing. I marched into the nearest tobacconist shop and somehow in stammering Italian bought four tickets for the water bus. I flounced out of the shop with my head held high. I would show that Geoffrey! I commanded my troops to follow me. Yes, I was bluffing. Not a clue.

I looked up and down the busy canal, filled with apprehension, then blindly decided which stop we should wait at, found the machine and managed to validate our tickets at a swipe machine. Yes, you read that correctly, but let me repeat it in case you missed it. I validated our tickets at a swipe machine. Don't ask me how; it must've been dumb luck but I pretended I knew exactly what I was doing. This let us enter a floating pontoon complete with all our carry-on-sized suitcases. And wonder of wonders, it was the right line and going to the right place. Praise the Lord; someone up above must have been helping me.

There was quite a crowd but we managed to get on the next boat, which had standing room only. Wedged shoulder to shoulder with our fellow tourists, we stood trying to hang on and keep hold of our suitcases. I glanced out of the window and was immediately hooked; it was just magical: the light playing on the water, the sun and shadows dancing as we sailed past majestic palazzos framed by striped pontoons, gondoliers in their blue and white stripes, happy faces gliding past on flotillas of brightly coloured craft. Oh, and there was Geoffrey, his features set like stone.

Alas, up ahead was our stop. Yes, I even knew where to get off. Oh how I loved Google. We hopped off at the Rialto Bridge. Well, not so much hopped but staggered and heaved our way off. I gave Geoffrey the hotel printout with instructions and a small map on the front for walking to the hotel and we set off with him leading the way. We were lost within nanoseconds.

We followed one route along a canal-side, only for it to end, and unless we wanted to swim across, we had to retrace our steps. We entered the maze of inner canals of the most beautiful emerald green;

it was shady here out of the sun. We trundled along single file beside canals, along little cobbled lanes, through piazzas and over tiny arched bridges. The latter were the worst; our suitcase wheels were making enough of a racket on the cobbles but going up the steps of a bridge was a rumble, rumble, thwack, rumble, rumble, thwack to the top, then on the way down it was thunk, thunk, thunk times four. It was an incredibly invasive and jarring sound. After we went through the same piazza for the third time, we stopped to have a think. Sweat dripped off our faces. Tempers were frayed.

'Oh,' I said, turning the page over in Geoffrey's hand. 'There's this bigger map here if that's any help.'

Geoffrey turned bright red. The scarlet-faced Gruffalo grumbled and I thought he was going to blow a gasket. A bead of sweat dropped onto the map.

Jan and Don rolled their eyes. Geoffrey exhaled deeply and turned his attention back to the map. It turned out we'd passed the hotel four times and had we not been off trekking for the best part of an hour, we would have reached it five minutes from the boat. But what an awesome place to be lost. It was fantastic with all the little canals, the hidden piazzas, the glass shops, the ornate carnival masks staring out from tiny boutiques, the gondolas gliding by, the music playing, Geoffrey's stony profile. I didn't care.

Donatella, the hotel manageress, was waiting for us as most of their guests apparently got lost. Later we heard her on the phone to some Americans and she sent her husband, Michelangelo, off to find them and lead them in.

'They sound like the Teenage Mutant Ninja Turtles,' muttered Don. 'They'll probably return with Raphael and Leonardo via a secret labyrinth of Ninja-Turtle underground drains.'

'Shush.' I nudged him, though it didn't stop us nicknaming the couple the Ninja Turtles for the rest of our stay.

What a wonderful hotel. It was huge, with canal views overlooking the gondola route and five minutes to Saint Mark's Square. It really was grand, with sumptuous furnishings and antiques. Even Geoffrey was impressed. I felt better about the amount of euros those turtles were sucking out of me. How appropriate that the Ninja Turtles were living right on top of a mass of watery drains.

We had a rest and some dinner that we brought with us after I secretly paid the €50 to open the oven without Geoffrey seeing. With the shutters open, all we could hear were gondolas going past, Italian singers and musicians on board playing guitars and piano accordions. They were singing such infectious, traditional Italian songs to the applause from the crowds of appreciative tourists gathered on the little arched bridge below. The magic of Venice had me in its grip and was starting to win Geoffrey over.

After dinner we went for a wander down to the gondola stop and I decided I was definitely going on one, no matter how much it rocked. On we went before I could change my mind. It was OK getting on but getting off would be another story. It was night-time so very mysterious and exciting gliding along through the quiet canals, with just the splash of the oars, the water lapping and the sound of the gondoliers' sing-song voices calling out to each other. Lights shone from within centuries-old palazzo windows, giving us a brief glimpse of the secret lives inside as we quietly glided by in the darkness.

Suddenly we popped out of a tiny, dark canal into the Grand Canal and were enveloped into a world of twinkling lights reflecting on the water from all the canal-side restaurants and flotillas of boats of all sizes rushing past: delivery boats, water buses, water taxis and private boats. We floated down the Grand Canal in absolute awe of the spectacle all around us; it was magnificent. Tourists watching from bridges photographed us and it felt glorious; one of those moments in life that we'll always remember.

And then the moment I'd been dreading arrived; it was time to get out of the gondola and it was the very opposite of glorious. The kids hopped off like agile little elks. Geoffrey had to remain seated at the back as ballast while I skipped gracefully off. In your dreams, sunshine. I'm large, have zero balance and a buggered foot. I stood up and things went pear-shaped.

I took a step and the boat leant. I reacted by staggering in the opposite direction. The boat tipped with me and soon we were swaying together in perfect synchrony in some sort of terrifying and clumsy dance. The gondolier looked panicked as he desperately tried to hold the gondola against the mooring without it capsizing. He yelled at the bambinos to help their mama off his gondola. In Italian I think it was more like 'get this crazy woman off my boat'. Geoffrey smirked unhelpfully.

GYPSIES AND THIEVES

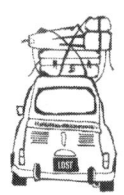

So much for not eating out in Venice. My €50 kitchen didn't include a toaster and we were out of milk. So we ate breakfast beside the Grand Canal on the other side of the Rialto Bridge. Surprisingly for such a tourist hotspot, the breakfast wasn't overpriced and the food and service were good. Geoffrey was expecting the staff to be jaded by the never-ending procession of tourists but he had to admit that everyone was friendly, helpful and welcoming.

We crossed back over the bridge and carried on walking the Grand Canal along the other side before heading into the interior canals, window shopping and exploring. As I approached a little bridge crossing a small canal, a gypsy posing as a tourist with a camera around his neck was sitting on the step of the bridge. I did a double take, but yes, his hand was going very, very slowly into the handbag of a lady standing on the bridge taking photos. The foolish woman had her bag wide open and was of course distracted taking pictures of the canal. I looked around. Nope, no Ninja Turtles waiting to come to the rescue so I would have to do.

'Stop right there!' I shouted and giving him a withering look, pointed directly at his face. 'I'm watching you, buster.' His hand jerked back out again and he legged it. If I'd thought of it at the time, I would've shouted 'Cowabunga!' in true Ninja-Turtle style.

In the afternoon we walked into Saint Mark's Square to tour the basilica with our prepaid, skip-the-queue voucher. And what a magnificent square it was with Saint Mark's Basilica, Campanile and the Doge's Palace at one end and the Clock Tower, Correr Museum, palazzos and the long arcade making up the huge, rectangular space. As we were about to enter, some pompous woman tried to stop me.

'Join the line like everyone else,' she hissed.

I explained politely that we had prepaid vouchers and could go in. All heads in the substantial queue looked accusingly at us. The woman snapped that we couldn't jump the queue.

'Whatever, lady, we're going in,' I replied.

'They won't let you,' she barked.

'Watch me,' I said and in we marched, past the line to the ticket turnstile. I showed the man our vouchers and we were admitted. I resisted the urge to raise a smug finger at the glaring eyes behind me. *All you need is Google, lady.*

The visit was more interesting because it was an exceptionally high tide and water was now rushing into the square and the cathedral. Before we could enter, we waited while the staff quickly assembled the stacks of raised boardwalks which we'd seen all around the place. Now we knew what they were for. Then we were able to walk in on top of these planks above the water. It was stunningly beautiful inside and staggeringly huge; the mosaic ceilings all in gold hues were amazing, as was the floor, despite it being partially submerged under tidal Venice.

When we came out, we crossed the square, which was crowded with tourists and exuding a lively, happy atmosphere. Classical music echoed from all the restaurants around it. We went into the museum ticket office to exchange another of my prepaid vouchers for tickets to the Doge's Palace for the following day. I approached the counter and the gentleman serving me suddenly twitched violently and shouted, 'Go f#@% your mother's dog and stick it up your fat arse.'

Jan's and Don's eyes bulged out on stalks.

'But Nana doesn't have a dog,' said Don, ever the stickler for the facts. Jan glared at her brother. 'Just saying.' He shrugged.

I grinned awkwardly, silently waiting for some sort of social cue to come to mind; nope, I had nothing. Tirade of abuse finished, the gentleman shook himself and said, 'Oooh, that was a good one,' and carried on as though nothing had happened. Ah, we all realised he had Tourette's and admired him immensely for the way he handled it.

That night we headed into Saint Mark's Square where we saw the glow in the dark of the little toy plastic helicopters flying high in the sky. I found one of the Bangladeshi men selling them and asked for two.

'Five,' he said.

'No, two.'

'I'll give you a good price for ten,' he insisted, pulling them out and trying to shove them at me.

'No, I'm only buying two,' I repeated firmly.

'I'll give you a whole bag for €10.'

'Right, that's it,' I said very firmly. 'I can buy two or I can buy none. Your choice.'

After that we were firm friends; boundaries had been set and he knew just how far I could be pushed.

We were happily enjoying the helicopters whooshing high in the air, lighting up the square, when more and more gypsy pedlars decided we were the night's target. This was because we were the only tourists brave (or stupid) enough to stand in the middle of Saint Mark's Square at night and deal with the harassment. Other visitors stuck to the perimeters along the arcade in full light by the shops and restaurants and watched with interest.

I didn't mind being offered a rose but when I respectfully declined it, that should've been the end of things. A particularly determined rose seller had failed in his attempts to shove one in my hands so he deftly attached the rose firmly to my handbag then demanded money for it. That was crossing a line as far as I was concerned. I looked him right in the eyes and said, 'You can remove it or I will stomp on it. Your choice.' My Bangladeshi friend chuckled; he knew I meant business. The pesky rose seller obviously thought I was bluffing and again demanded the cash. Quick as a flash, I had that rose off my bag and under my foot. He let out a string of expletives at me in a foreign language. The rest of the rose pedlars realised they were wasting their time and moved on.

On our last day, we were woken by the workers leaving on their boats then all the service boats going past: rubbish collection on a barge, delivery of clean laundry, fruit and vegetables all came trundling up the canal past the window. I found it fascinating and spent the dawn hours hanging out of the window while sipping my cup of tea, my only company the two pigeons cooing to me perched on a window box across the canal. I was soaking it all up and never wanted it to end.

We spent our last morning touring the Doge's Palace which was full of obscene amounts of gold and impressively oversized and ornate works of art. Culturally overloaded, I led the way down the back alleys to a small restaurant I'd researched on TripAdvisor. And who was sitting next to us? The gondoliers all on their lunch break, a room full of tanned, muscle-bound Italian men in tight, striped T-shirts. What was not to like? Adele came on the radio singing 'Someone Like You' and the gondoliers joined in. The little restaurant reverberated to the sound of their deep baritone voices. When we left, people were waiting outside to get a table. It was well priced; the pasta dishes we ate were delicious and the people were lovely. Geoffrey had to admit I'd done my research well.

We rode the water bus down the Grand Canal for our last night in Venice before returning to Saint Mark's Square. After a gelato, Geoffrey and Don went into the middle of the square to fly their plastic, glow-in-the-dark helicopters. Jan and I treated ourselves to a seat in one of the cafés along the arcade with the posh people and watched them with a wine.

Meanwhile every pedlar in the vicinity descended on Geoffrey and tried to sell him more helicopters. We laughed, watching and waiting. They circled him like sharks waiting for the kill; the poor things hadn't heard about Geoffrey's temper tantrums. Then the prey bit back, screaming, 'All of you just bugger off before I ram a helicopter up your backsides.' The pedlars took a step back, considering their next move. The diners seated along the outdoor arcade fell silent. Jan and I stifled our laughter.

Suddenly a forecast thunderstorm hit. It was fantastic: torrential rain and howling wind. The waiters rushed to assist Jan and me to relocate further back under cover. The tourists dispersed in a hurry. Geoffrey and Don headed for our table while we downed our glasses of wine and the rose pedlars scuttled back to lurk in the shadows. Within seconds they'd ditched the roses and helicopters and were back selling umbrellas.

We hurriedly pulled our raincoats from the backpack. It was great visually, seeing the lightning flashing above Saint Mark's Square, lighting up the cathedral and the Clock Tower, and hearing the thunder booming. Lightning illuminated the canal as we made our way home to Ninja HQ in the pouring rain with no one around. The raindrops cascaded in sheets into the canals, creating a magnificent plopping sound, and rain sashayed across the marble cobbles, making our return journey very slow.

The gondoliers scurried for cover. The tourists had vanished; we were alone in the storm, splashing our way canal-side back to our hotel. One of the Ninja Turtles was in the doorway waiting to let us in, laughing at our bedraggled, dripping appearance. We were exhilarated. We headed upstairs to drape wet clothes, sit in our PJs and watch the storm through the shutters. I didn't ever want to leave Venice. I was so glad I'd risked breaking the ban and that the Venetians weren't all pretentious prats as Geoffrey had predicted.

MY PELVIC FLOOR MUSCLES NEED TIGHTENING

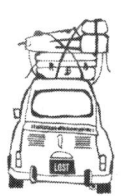

Our exit from Venice was less stressful than our arrival. We retrieved the car from the garage where they were still guarding it so well that they didn't want us to take it. La La was pleased to see us and performed excellently, getting us safely out of Venice and heading out of Italy towards Dubrovnik in Croatia. Don said something from the back seat about us being in Slovenia shortly. That got my attention and I sat up straight.

'What d'you mean we'll be in Slovenia? Is that part of Croatia?' I asked.

'God, Mum, you need to study a map,' he said. 'It's a separate country.'

'Shit!' I exclaimed. 'I hope we don't need a visa. Does anyone know if you need a visa to enter Slovenia?'

'Oh for God's sake,' said Geoffrey, looking bemused.

I must've been so busy googling Venice that this bit had escaped my attention. Geoffrey fiddled about with La La's satnav map to move it forward a bit and yep, there was Slovenia in my way of getting to Croatia. Nothing ruffles a super-planner more than an unexpected country appearing from nowhere.

As we approached, I was filled with apprehension so it was with great relief that we sallied forth unchecked into the Republic of Slovenia. My relief was short-lived as we needed to stop for petrol and lunch. I leant over and yanked Don's earphones out.

'What currency do they use? What language do they speak?' I gibbered at him.

With a roll of his eyes, he Googled it. 'Euros and Slovenian,' he informed me before re-inserting his earphones. We had euros, phew, and not knowing the language was nothing new. I was horrified that all this could have escaped my normally super-organised self.

A hundred kilometres later, we arrived at a Croatian border control. The chief planner hadn't even thought about border crossings, just assumed you drove in and out unchecked like between France and Italy. How was I supposed to know they were a bit more fussy here? We were waved through with a smile upon sight of our New Zealand passports and headed onto an eerily deserted autoroute, very new-looking and modern, just no other cars around.

To add to the eerie atmosphere, a storm broke over us when we were high up in forest-covered hills that looked very much like the Yukon in Canada. As we climbed higher, fog surrounded us and our vision was reduced to about five metres, forcing us to crawl along. On a positive note, there was no chance of another vehicle rear-ending us in the thick fog as there weren't any other cars around. As we descended into the valley, the scenery was beautiful with golden, orange and red trees wearing their autumn colours, and signs warning to watch out for bears on the road. What? Did I read that correctly? Yes, there was another one.

'BEARS!' I shouted out to tell the kids.

Then La La decided to mix it up with a bit of off-road touring, on a road that was so minor it was more ruts and dirt than road. I opened a bag of limoncello-filled chocolates. Phew, they were strong. I felt I needed fortification for whatever La La had up her sleeve. What she had planned was an off-road trip back in time, winding through remote Croatian villages with people out tending their crops by hand in the fields or ploughing using a horse. Most of the stone, chalet-style homes seemed to have a cow and a goat tied up outside. We came to villages which had been all but destroyed during the Croatian War of Independence in the '90s.

The kids' earphones were out. We saw the effects of war first hand as we passed house after house with roofs imploded by mortar shelling, windows blasted out and fire damage visible. With ties to the land, most families appeared to have simply rebuilt next to their original home, leaving the old one as a lasting reminder of what had happened during the years of civil war. This was a very sobering but fascinating drive through history. Had it not been for La La, we would have driven along the new road without seeing or learning.

La La now had a front-seat passenger called Tipsy. I was feeling quite merry by now after consuming the best part of a bag of limoncello-filled liqueurs.

We finally arrived at our hotel in the Plitvice Lakes National Park around 5 p.m. in pouring rain, where we stayed overnight before carrying on to Dubrovnik the next morning.

It was still stormy when we left and we drove through more beautiful scenery, vast wilderness areas with no sign of mankind but great for bears. With a sense of déjà vu, we suddenly came to another border post.

'Oh shit. What country are we going into this time, Don?' I asked.

'Read the sign,' said the smart-arse in the back.

Bosnia apparently. I didn't dare ask if it was part of Croatia. The dour, sour-faced Bosnian dude demanded passports and papers for our car. Suddenly the stupid diesel vehicle did its random trick; the car revved loudly and leapt forward like we were flooring it to escape. I got the giggles and the Bosnian jerked his head up and raised his eyebrows at us, finally happy he was finished with our papers, and we proceeded into Bosnia. The territory was noticeably run down and worn-looking; the roads were in worse condition, buildings dilapidated and cars old. We drove through Bosnia and out the other side, back through another border control into Croatia.

Mandarins were in season as we passed through a major fruit-growing region along the Neretva River delta so we stopped at one of many roadside stalls to buy a bag of them and some mandarin honey. Further on we pulled over and got out to admire the river valley below while munching on the deliciously sweet fruit. I made the mistake of opening the honey to taste it. What ensued amounted to four adults dancing like demented turkeys around a car park, chased by a tribe of man-eating Croatian wasps. Memories of the giant Asian hornets were fresh in our minds. The car, which held the only chance of escape, was now filled with buzzing balls of anger descending on our bag of mandarins. I hurled the honey over the bank and shut Geoffrey in the car to dispatch the enemy. Finally we made our getaway.

'It's the gypsy curse,' Don claimed from the back seat.

We arrived in Dubrovnik about 5 p.m. and found the apartment. Typical of anywhere I'd booked, we just looked around for the steepest, most difficult place to get to and assumed that would be where we were staying.

The apartment was halfway to heaven, the highest house in Dubrovnik, with wonderful views overlooking the old city. When we saw the driveway up to the house, Geoffrey said, 'Oh f#@%, not again.' The kids and I shut our eyes and prayed.

To get up such a steep incline with all the weight in the car, Geoffrey floored it. I heard screaming then realised it was coming from me. The car paused. I opened one eye then Geoffrey took a run at the last section to get us into our car park. With a huge rev and a wheel spin, we got onto the car parking pad with all of La La's sensor alarms furiously beeping as she detected the proximity to the concrete walls. Geoffrey proudly announced that he got all three sensors into the red zone at once like it was a GOOD THING! I think I peed my pants.

Once we'd recovered and got inside, the apartment itself was stunning, with the most amazing view I've ever seen. The balcony looked over the Adriatic Sea with Lokrum Island in the distance and the old city of Dubrovnik below us, encircled by its defensive stone walls. We were in the perfect position to watch the sunset over a glass of wine. That evening we spent our time catching up on emails and Facebook while Geoffrey planned a day trip to visit Mostar in Bosnia and Herzegovina before we left. He got busy on Google maps and made plans. Little did we know that we would put our lives at risk.

GIVE US A FAG, SARGE

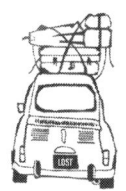

Mostar, a historic town on the Neretva River, is known for being more Turkish/Muslim than Bosnian. The colours hit us first as we wandered down a cobblestoned street leading towards the river, bordered on either side by stalls selling swathes of pashminas, Turkish rugs, Turkish tea sets, copper and a myriad of Turkish lamps made with a rainbow of mosaic glass. Stall holders called out to us and each other. Islamic music came from the back streets and the call to prayer echoed around.

As we continued towards the Neretva River, the Stari Most, a rebuilt, stone-arched, 16th-century Ottoman bridge appeared in front of us and it really was remarkable. We climbed up its steeply cobbled gradient to the top and down the other side. The river was a deep-emerald green and the old town on the opposite bank was just as picture perfect. There were fantastic shopping bargains to be had using the local currency of convertible marks. Everything was cheap and very much like being in a Turkish bazaar. The architecture was quite different to what we'd seen in Croatia, with a darker, bluish-grey stone and a backdrop of towering mosque spires. While Jan and I were distracted purchasing beautiful Turkish lamps of mosaic-coloured glass, Geoffrey and Don were arming themselves with a large souvenir dagger, not knowing that this dagger would feature in two scary incidents.

We left Mostar about 3 p.m. and Geoffrey insisted on going the long route on one of his adventurous, scenic drives, which irrevocably reversed our tides of luck. We took the road following the River Trebišnjica and as we drove through a vast valley bordered with sheer, rocky mountains, there were no signs of civilisation at all. Mutterings came from the back seat wondering where on earth Dad was driving us and how long this was going to take. I felt uneasy for some reason and couldn't relax or enjoy the beauty of the scenery.

I asked Jan to pass me a mandarin. I reached my hand back to grab it just as a car came flying around the next bend at high speed, spun out of control and continued its inevitable trajectory towards us. There was no avoiding it. No one spoke. From the moment we saw the car coming directly at us until impact was probably only four seconds. I think we all thought the same thing: 'We're going to die.' Geoffrey braked and swerved to the right as much as he could before the inevitable impact. BANG. The mandarin smashed into the back of my seat. Don said afterwards he thought about the horrible TV ad at home in New Zealand showing a family and a piece of fruit flying forward on impact in a crash. Now here we were, seemingly re-enacting the scene as mandarins flew around the car.

There's no describing the noise or suddenness of stopping upon impact or the force of being thrown forward; they're brutal. The collision pushed our car backwards by about six metres, shunting it half over the side of the bank with me on the down side and the vehicle supported by a thorny hedge. I was aware of an immediate pain in my chest as I quickly glanced behind me to check the kids were OK. Don and Jan scrambled through the upper door. Smoke poured from the other car and I was terrified it was going to burst into flames. Geoffrey came round and balanced on the prickly hedge to get me out.

I rushed to hug my children; nothing else mattered. Jan noticed my neck was bleeding and wiped at the blood with her hands. We assessed our injuries, which were relatively minor considering what had just happened: whiplash, chest and leg bruising and minor cuts. There was a bitingly cold wind so we quickly put coats on as I was concerned about shock. Jan's hands were shaking and her voice wavering. Don was taking it all in his stride. Little did we know that there was worse to come.

Geoffrey tried to communicate with the two men from the other car who were a father and son. The son, who would have been in his twenties, knew a little English so he acted as interpreter for us as best he could. He'd called the police, who were coming from Trebinje, about an hour away. They were both OK, considering the state of their car, thanks to airbags. I asked what had happened but it was obvious he'd been going too fast around the corner and lost control. Later the son did a disappearing act, leaving his father to deal with the consequences and to pretend to the police that he'd been driving.

Geoffrey found his cell phone in the debris and rang the rental company helpline to report the accident. They said someone would call us back; a call that never came. We were on our own.

As we looked around, we realised we were in the middle of nowhere next to the Andusic vineyard and some sheep-grazing land. Some men appeared from the only visible building and beckoned for the kids and me to go with them, taking us to a little bar. Inside, it was tiny and hazy, with a handful of local men drinking and smoking in a bar the size of a standard front room. All conversation stopped as we entered and everyone stared at us. They showed us in and we sat down as they produced hot coffee for all of us and a red wine for me.

The locals greeted us, shook our hands warmly and conversation resumed. They fussed over Don wearing shorts and getting cold and insisted we sit by the fire, communicating with gestures.

'It's the gypsy curse again,' said Don.

Well we can't be that cursed, I thought as ironically, with all that deserted landscape out there, we'd managed to crash outside a small bar.

It took well over an hour for three Bosnian police officers to arrive. One of them spoke a little English but dismissed us with an impatient wave of the hand when we tried to say anything. They were abrupt and arrogant and marched around, guns in holsters. They didn't ask if anyone was hurt or try to find out what had happened. Our biggest fear was that as foreigners in a country well known for its corrupt police force, we would be blamed and asked for money or worse. They took photos and began taking measurements. We returned to wait with our friends in the bar while this was going on.

Finally, after about two hours, the police came in and sat with the father of the other car driver for a coffee and managed to convey to us that transport was on the way. The fact that they were having a coffee with the father of the man who'd caused the accident was concerning. We were vulnerable, at their mercy.

We sat quietly, subdued, tired and hungry. Eventually when it was dark, the tow truck arrived with an ancient car on the back. One of the policemen opened the boot and motioned for us to put our belongings in and get into the car, without speaking a single word to us. Geoffrey, Jan and Don got in the back with some of our gear piled on their laps and I climbed in the front. The officer returned and started the engine.

We headed off into the night, not a light to be seen; we were totally isolated, both geographically and linguistically.

Lightning flickered and lit up the sky ominously in the mountains across the valley. We were alone with a Bosnian police officer and my eyes rested on the gun around his waist. We didn't know where we were being taken or how corrupt the police might be. We were tourists with money and passports and were in an isolated area with no witnesses and no one knew where we were. The horrifying implication hit me and I felt sick. Was he going to shoot us all at the side of the road? As if to confirm my worst fears, he started randomly slowing down like he was looking for somewhere to stop. I later found out that Jan was thinking the very same thing and was feeling around in the back seat for the souvenir dagger that Don had bought in Mostar. For once his bloody daggers might have been of use.

Finally the police officer stopped in a dark area. I wanted to scream but decided I wasn't going down without a fight. I searched in the darkness for my walking stick and got a good grip, ready to smash him over the head if he went for his gun. Jan readied the dagger. He reached in his other pocket, not the gun side, and pulled out a cell phone and made a call, all in Bosnian. Then he started the engine again and we drove on. Every muscle in my body was tense and my heart was racing. I thought the drive would never end and we must've been in that car for about an hour. He didn't speak a single word to us. Just a smile or a nod would've made such a difference. He showed no humanity at all. I don't think I've felt so vulnerable in all my life or ever seriously questioned the wisdom of taking our children travelling.

I finally saw the lights of a town in the distance and felt hugely relieved as we drove into Trebinje. We pulled into a large police compound with guards at the gate which then slammed shut behind us. We were trapped. We drove in and stopped outside a three-storey, concrete-block building. The police officer got out without saying a word then motioned for us to do so. But then he strode off and just left us standing in the freezing cold, teeth chattering, while he went to talk to some other officers who came out to stare at us. I noticed the guards were all wearing Soviet Army-style ushanka fur hats teamed with dark-coloured trench coats and black boots. The officer beckoned to us to, 'Come, come,' and he marched off towards the building.

He led us into a big, cold, dimly lit building, upstairs and along a corridor smelling of urine. The noise of our shoes on the old lino seemed so loud in the silent, empty place. We arrived in a corridor where there was a desk at one end, lit by a single light bulb dangling from the ceiling. An officer was typing on an ancient computer on what looked like a wooden school desk. The alleged driver of the other car was sitting there and didn't look up at us. We were taken into a side room and the officer pointed at seats. He said nothing but started typing with two fingers at the old computer.

There we sat, in our little holding pen, listening to the old clock on the wall tick on and on, not knowing what was happening. The kids seemed to grasp the seriousness of the situation and remained silent. Nobody offered us food or water. Don leant against the wall, nodding off, and Jan huddled next to me. I put my arm through hers, the closeness providing support. Geoffrey waited on the chair opposite us, looking grey. At no point did anyone ask if we were OK or required medical attention. I felt anxious but kept a lid on it because I needed to be calm for the kids. Jan's hands were still shaking.

The officer took the driver's statement first but it was all done in Bosnian so we had no idea what he might be saying. Then it was our turn. Another officer asked for our passports, took them and left the room. Geoffrey and I exchanged looks. We were waiting for them to try and extort money from us but it didn't happen; that would come later but from a different source.

About 3 a.m. the phone rang, causing us all to jump. They said a taxi was there and we were free to go when they were finished with our statement. The officers returned our passports to us, produced a statement written in Cyrillic and ordered us to sign it. We weren't offered any translation of what it said but sign it we did because we desperately wanted to get out of there. We needed no encouragement to leave. We practically sprinted down the stairs to the waiting taxi.

Travel isn't always a bed of roses; sometimes those rose-tinted glasses get smashed up a bit.

HOW MAY WE NOT HELP YOU?

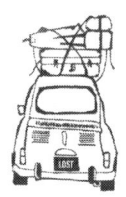

*A*fter a sleepless night, we were up early.

'I can't believe how useless the car rental company was yesterday,' I said. 'I thought a French company would be better than that,' I said.

'They were really *merde* (shit),' Don agreed.

Geoffrey emailed Merde Motors with the details of the accident and photos clearly showing the damage before ringing them to organise a replacement car. So began our Merde Motors nightmares.

He explained that we needed a car urgently as it was Friday and we were due to depart Croatia on the overnight ferry on Sunday to continue our holiday in the Abruzzo, Italy. So could they ring the local branch in Dubrovnik and organise a car?

'That is not possible, sir. We cannot start to organise a replacement car until we get the police report,' was the answer.

'But the police report is in Bosnia. I can't collect it without a car.'

'We cannot proceed without the police report. When you get it, you need to scan it and send it to us,' they replied, not budging an inch.

Geoffrey's voice went up a notch. 'But I can't *get* the report. I *don't* have a *car*. I also don't travel with a scanner on me.'

'Scan it at the police station,' was Merde Motors's reply.

Geoffrey snorted. 'They barely have any light bulbs, never mind a scanner.'

'Call us when you have the police report, sir,' and they hung up.

'Arrogant French frogs,' screamed Geoffrey and went to lie down with a headache.

I apologise to all the lovely French people out there, except the ones at the call centre. After fuming for some time, I rang Merde Motors Arse-istance myself. I could be a lot narkier than Geoffrey when required. I asked if they could organise a car to take Geoffrey to Bosnia to get the police report but in the meantime could they at least call the local car dealer and book us one so that we could be assured of having a vehicle once they got their precious report?

'No, we cannot, *madame*.'

Patience exhausted, I snapped like a tight rubber band. Things got heated and I told them exactly what I thought of their customer service. Five minutes later a man rang back and grudgingly informed me that they would give Geoffrey a ride on their tow truck at 7:30 a.m. next day to the Bosnian police station to get the report and they would bring the car back on the truck.

'Well that's all well and good,' I said. 'But what about our replacement car?'

'No report, no car,' was the response and he hung up.

After another restless night, Geoffrey and I were up early, nursing our coffee in silence on the balcony. It was a beautiful morning with the rooftops of Dubrovnik old town glowing red in the sunrise below our apartment high on the hill. A cruise ship drifted into view on the calm waters. *If we'd travelled on a cruise ship or bus tour like normal people, none of this would've happened.* I wondered what it would be like: everything organised for you, never getting lost. I quickly dismissed the thought; all our adventures, both good and bad, usually eventuated out of things going wrong.

Geoffrey was hesitant about returning to the police station in Bosnia, not knowing what it was we'd signed. For all we knew, they might've been about to throw him in the slammer. We agreed it was better if the kids and I remained behind. He made sure his cell phone was fully charged and took extra cash in case he needed it before dashing down to the bottom of the hill to await his tow-truck pickup.

A text came in from Geoffrey a couple of hours later. The report had been ready and waiting for him. The documents were all stamped and signed and he was free to go. They loaded the car on the truck and they were on their way back.

A further text said he'd been detained at the border crossing as the Bosnian border guards were being difficult. We waited nervously, wondering if he would get out safely. The kids and I sat staring at the phone. Finally it beeped; Geoffrey was through but they'd blackmailed him. The tow-truck driver had acted as interpreter as the dictatorial customs official stomped back and forth to his office, each time coming back to imply they were missing some fictitious stamp. The driver explained that this happened all the time. The officer wanted cash; an amount was to be placed inside the passport and handed over. If it wasn't enough, it would be passed back with the money still in it and Geoffrey would have to add more. If it came back empty, then they could go.

Geoffrey asked what sort of amount was normal and the driver said they usually only extorted €10-20 from undesirable locals but for a tourist he would want more. Geoffrey tried €50. The official accepted it and returned the passport, minus the cash. Suddenly they didn't need another stamp; they were free to go.

In the absence of a 'do your scanning here' shop at the side of a rural Bosnian road while riding in a tow truck, Geoffrey photographed the report on his phone and emailed it to Merde Motors when he got back to the apartment later. 'Ha, good luck reading that, you froggy bastards,' he said triumphantly as he pressed the 'send' button. We looked at him enquiringly. 'The police report is all written in Cyrillic,' he said and we all chortled with smug glee. Classic. They would finally get their precious police report and not be able to read a word of it.

Happy in the knowledge that now, with said report in hand, they would finally organise our rental car, Geoffrey rang to confirm that he'd done as asked.

'Sir, we will order you a taxi,' they said.

Breathing deeply, Geoffrey once again patiently explained why we needed a rental car, *not* a taxi. They agreed to organise it and call us back by 3 p.m. with the details. This left them with five hours to make a phone call and arrange a car. Simple stuff, right? No, of course not. That's someone else's book, where travel is all sunshine and skipping through daisies.

Naturally 3 p.m. came and went and we didn't hear back from them. We were due to depart in the morning and as yet had no car. What were we supposed to do? The local dealership would be closing very soon.

I was on the phone to Merde Motors again.

'Oh that's right, you need a taxi to Bosnia,' the operator said.

I groaned out loud and looked for the nearest wall to bang my head against. 'No, I do *not* want a taxi to Bosnia. I never wish to set foot in Bosnia again in my life. We're waiting for a rental car to go to Split in the morning.'

There was a pause while she brought the details up on her screen.

'Have you managed to ring the local Merde Motors dealer given you've now had five hours to do so?' I asked.

'No, madam, you do not understand,' came the condescending voice of someone dealing with an idiot. 'It is not that easy. We are in France. You are in another country. We would have to make a toll call. I emailed them.'

I couldn't believe what I was hearing. Taking a deep breath and sounding completely exasperated I said, 'I know you're in another country because we've had to keep calling you lot in France on our cell phone every time you fail to ring us back. Are you actually serious?' Barely stopping for breath, I continued. 'It's only hours till our departure so surely you sitting back hoping someone will reply isn't the wisest course of action. Maybe, just perhaps, you could pick up the phone and use it please. I need a car to be on our doorstep in an hour or you'll be hearing from me again.'

She started to snivel.

No, I'm not proud of myself but my message got through; a

telephone was used for the purposes of swift and efficient communication and within the hour the local dealer delivered a car to our door. Now there was still the issue of the vehicle to meet us at Ancona in Italy. I was now banned from ringing the call centre by some officious little twit of a man so Geoffrey was left to sort that bit out. They said we would have to get a taxi from the port into the city to the car dealer, which was fine with us.

As we headed to the port the following day, I proudly informed the kids that I'd booked us on the *Marco Polo* ship for our overnight trip. It was the pride of the Jadrolinija fleet and would be just like going on a cruise.

'We have a four-berth cabin,' I said. 'Luxury.' We'd never been on a ferry with cabins to sleep in so this was exciting.

While we were waiting to board, we got a text from Merde Motors saying that we now had to get a taxi 50 kilometres to an entirely different city to get a car. No reason given of course. But it was too late even to contemplate arguing with them. We were boarding a ship and had no Wi-Fi.

'That's your fault for making them cry,' muttered Geoffrey.

People stared at the four of us trudging in single file across the wharf to the international ferry terminal dragging four large suitcases, four small suitcases, a moonboot, a laptop bag, two large handbags, a backpack and two bags of accumulated groceries; we looked like pack mules. We then had to lug it all through the boat and up a flight of stairs to the accommodation level. I inwardly cursed Merde Motors with every step as we should've been driving on board with our luggage stowed comfortably in our car overnight. A kind-hearted ferry worker standing in the cargo hold took one look at what we were attempting to drag on board up the rusty old ramp and came to assist, taking from me the biggest of the bags and escorting us to a large cargo lift. I remain very grateful. I was acutely aware of just how little luggage everyone else had.

About 30 seconds after we boarded, I realised that this was no luxury cruise ship and if this was the pride of the fleet then the rest of them must've been at the bottom of the ocean. It was like stepping back in time to the '70s, all fake brown wood veneer, orange and red carpet and rust, lots of rust. A hostess led us down the corridor in single file to our cabin. I remained hopeful, until I saw how close together each cabin door was.

Geoffrey was up front and opened the door, peering in. He and Don laughed. Jan and I couldn't see what they were sniggering at. It was some time till we got to the door as they couldn't fit inside the room. Geoffrey entered, dragging his bags, and Don tried to follow but apparently that was as deep as the room was. As he came to a halt, we remained stuck out in the corridor. I doubled over laughing. A man came along behind us and I offered to move everything aside to let him through. He said no, he preferred to wait and watch as it was pretty entertaining.

Grumbling away to himself, Geoffrey ordered Don to stand on a bunk while he started to pile bags on top of each other up to the ceiling, then Jan was able to enter, directed to stand in the minuscule toilet cubicle out of the way. Finally it was my turn to shove my bags forward and look in the cabin. Despite expecting it to be tiny, I was still shocked that anything expected to sleep four people could be *that* small. Geoffrey ordered me onto a bunk and finally he was able to close the door, but not before the gentleman waiting behind us glanced in and grinned.

To get sorted we worked out a system of taking turns to stand up one at a time as there was only room for one person to move. The bathroom was a horror: a basin smaller than a piece of A4 paper with a toilet next to it and a shower nozzle over the toilet; rust and three decades of grime encrusted every paint-peeling surface. As I discovered later, the cubicle was so small that to wipe your bottom your head banged into the door, forcing you to arrange your eye socket carefully around the rusted door handle. Not being skilled in contortionism, no one showered; we had a sponge-down that night.

We all lay on our bunks, looked at each other and laughed and laughed. It was just so far from the picture I'd painted in our minds.

After days of stress, our humour and the ability to see the funny side of things broke back through and we all thoroughly enjoyed our night. It was just too comical for words. A gin in the fresh air on deck as I watched the lights of Croatia fade away into the distance chased away the claustrophobic confines of the cabin. Once we got out to sea somewhere between Croatia and Italy on the Adriatic Sea, the ship started to rock a bit. I took a sleeping pill, sighed and wondered what the hell could go wrong next.

I didn't have long to wait. Upon arrival in Ancona at 7 a.m., the lift broke, meaning we had to lug all twelve bags and a moonboot down to the vehicle deck or wait in the queue while the lift was fixed. In the stairwell an Italian drama unfolded. I watched with interest as a group of elderly Italian nonnas on a pilgrimage shoved their way to the front of the sizeable queue for the lift. The other passengers were having none of it and an old man took the nonnas to task. And so it began, the arm-waving, dramatic gestures, raised voices and shouting, but no way were the nonnas backing down. It seemed they had God on their side. This was proven when the priest travelling with them arrived, squeezing firmly through the crowd to stand stoically beside his flock.

After we'd dragged all our bags off the ferry, we flagged down a taxi big enough for all our assorted luggage and asked the driver to take us to Macerata to pick up our rental car. He paused and said, 'But that's another city; it's far away.' He shook his head and couldn't understand why we would need to drive to another city when there were plenty of rental cars in Ancona. Hard to explain Merde Motors organised this and did things differently to ordinary people. The taxi driver seemed to take this as a personal affront on the worthiness of Ancona's cars and drove us at 130 kilometres per hour to the neighbouring city of Macerata. We screeched to a halt outside a tiny dump of an office and he dumped our bags unceremoniously on the curb before he sped off, clutching his cash.

There was no sign of rental cars outside, just a broken and crumbly pavement on an extremely busy road. Geoffrey went in to talk to the man at the counter while we waited at the side of the road with the luggage, causing some passing curiosity; it was like a travelling circus had come to town. Geoffrey reappeared and announced that the car wasn't there. The agent locked his office and sped off. I just groaned and the kids grumbled.

'He's gone to get the car. He said he'll be ten minutes tops,' said Geoffrey.

'I need the loo,' I muttered.

'I want coffee,' said Jan.

'This sucks,' moaned Don.

'Shut up,' said Geoffrey.

'Better be a good car after all this shit,' I commented.

'Well this is what happens when you yell at frogs,' spat Geoffrey.

Twenty minutes later the agent returned, pulling up on the other side of the road in a dump of a car that was very definitely not of the rental car variety that we'd paid for.

'Oh God,' I muttered.

'Suck it up,' said Geoffrey and went in to sign the papers. He was gone for ages so we started to porter the luggage over the busy road one bag at a time, like a line of sherpas. Once we had everything over the other side, I opened the boot. We gave a collective groan. There was no way our luggage was going to fit in there.

We did our best, trying all different configurations. Some of the gathered bystanders joined in with the luggage version of the Rubik's Cube but it just wouldn't fit. So I ordered the kids into the back seat while I piled bags between and around them up to the roof, finally hopping in myself, weighed down by the overflow. Right, we were all set to head off to the Abruzzo. Now we just needed to set the satnav.

'Oh for God's sake,' said Geoffrey as we noticed the absence of one. There was also no map in the car or the office. I wanted to ring Merde Motors and scream at them further but Geoffrey wouldn't let me plus I was banned from calling them. I slumped down, defeated.

We had no way of knowing where we were or which way to go. The decision was taken out of our hands by the mountains of luggage blocking our rear view. We would drive straight on as there was zero visibility to turn around. Geoffrey was shouting. Jan needed coffee. I wanted to murder every single person working for Merde Motors and Don shoved his headphones in his ears.

'I never ever thought I would say this,' I said, 'but I really miss La La.'

'Yeah, poor La La,' agreed Don. 'We didn't even get to say goodbye to her after the car crash.'

'She's dead now,' said Jan.

'She was a bloody satnav and a useless one at that,' argued Geoffrey.

HOW A DAY AT THE SEASIDE ENDS AT A PRISON FOR THE MOST VIOLENT MAFIOSO IN ITALY

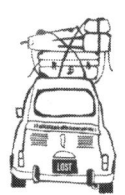

It was our third day in the beautiful Chieti region of the Abruzzo. Staying with Richard and Sarah in their beautiful stone home on the outskirts of Casoli was just what we needed. They were fantastic and attentive hosts; their residence was at one end of the enormous house and the other end was converted to a gorgeously luxurious and rustic holiday let. The first snow arrived with us and dusted the tops of the Maiella mountain range. The open fire, electric blankets and thick, cushiony duvets were perfect. The menagerie of cats was also most welcome, especially by the kids who were missing our pets so brought all the cats inside. It was a calm oasis for us to recover after the car crash and subsequent issues with the car rental company. The calmness didn't extend to beyond the gate unfortunately.

We planned to head to Guardiagrele, listed as one of the region's most beautiful medieval hilltop towns, then we would carry on to Roccascalegna village and castle. We'd already had two attempts at finding Guardiagrele, coming at it from two different angles, but both times it had eluded us. This time we were fully prepared. Geoffrey had done a Google search and studied our map. We were determined to find that wretched village, even though we were now without La La.

Back we went to the starting point in the next village, Civitella Messer Raimondo, where there was a signpost pointing to the elusive Guardiagrele. From there, five minutes later we came to a crossroads. No signpost for Guardiagrele, or anywhere else for that matter. I glanced sideways at Geoffrey, wondering if he was going to have a meltdown. We pulled over and consulted our map, deciding which road was the most likely.

'We're lost again, aren't we?' came a smart comment from the back seat.

We drove on, through many more such intersections, never coming to another signpost or any remotely navigational-looking object. Navigating by the stars would be as useful as anything else in these parts. An hour later we were stunned to arrive back at Casoli, the village ten minutes from where we'd set out.

'Are you serious?' groaned Geoffrey.

'Never mind, let's just head to Roccascalegna,' I said, hoping to avert a full-blown crisis.

Geoffrey continued to mutter quietly to himself about the local authorities spending too much time preening and sucking on olives to get any road signs put up.

We found what we thought was the right road and headed off, climbing upwards until we were winding around a narrow road along a ridge of hills with sweeping views across to the Maiella mountains. What followed was pretty much a repeat of the morning; same same but different, no form of signposts, nada, zip, zilch, zero.

Hours later, left in the darkness with rather dismal headlights after a scintillating day spent like mindless rodents on a treadmill, we searched for a way home. Our current, nondescript, rickety track culminated at the lights of a stone farmhouse and the car's headlights revealed a little old man out the front, sweeping up a massive pile of leaves from his drive. We came bouncing down the unpaved, narrow lane towards him. Geoffrey wound his window down and I used my very bad travel Italian to get across that we were lost. The gentleman conveyed his reply through gestures and rapid Italian to turn around and go back.

'What did he say?' asked Geoffrey.

'Get off my driveway, you total tossers,' I said, laughing. 'Well that's the impression I got anyway.'

Turning around was easier said than done given there was a big station wagon and a narrow, rutted lane in the dark. We three back-seat drivers cringed down in our seats, gritting our teeth and waiting for the usual crunch of Geoffrey hitting something. However the only crunch we heard was of the poor old boy's leaves as we drove right over the top of the pile he'd spent so long raking. He stood leaning on his rake, shaking his head. I was mortified and sank down even lower. We had no choice but to retrace our steps back through the town, along the top of the ridge over to Casoli then down to our village. It would take another hour or two at least. But I was very proud that my study of Italian had finally paid off and I was quite chuffed until Don replied, 'Personally I think your time would have been better spent studying maps.'

That broke the tension temporarily and we all had a good laugh as we headed towards home.

'But if you knew the way back, why didn't we just go that way in the first place?' asked Jan, completely exasperated.

'Well your father was taking us the quick route.'

'Daaaaad,' came the response from the back seat.

'You can shut up or get out,' fumed Dad.

'You can shut up or get out,' mimicked the kids in unison and the three of us all laughed, used to his harmless driving outbursts.

We finally made it home about half past ten that night, utterly exhausted and fed up after an entire day spent lost. We didn't find Roccascalegna until we tried again several days later. We couldn't wait to have a hot drink and some toast then climb upstairs and slip under the heavy duvets. I put a match to the gas cooker in the old kitchen while Jan and Don let the friendly cats in and Geoffrey lit the fire. There was a full moon glinting off the freshly fallen snow as I drew the curtains shut upstairs and turned on the electric blankets. The tiled floors felt cold underfoot; it was going to be a chilly night. I dispensed steaming cups of tea and coffee which the kids and I took upstairs to bed. We climbed in under the warmed-up sheets, finding comfort in being together, cats and all. I foolishly promised the kids a trip to the seaside the next day, with no getting lost and no mountain roads. We would stick to the main roads and make it there.

Finally everyone settled in for the night and all was quiet, but not for long. With everyone having been in our bed earlier, the slats had moved under the mattress. I rolled over and all the slats underneath me caved in and crashed to the floor. I was left slumped in a hole on my bed.

'Right, that's it,' moaned Geoffrey. 'You're nothing but trouble; what have you done now?'

I could do nothing but laugh while he pulled me out of the hole and fixed the bed. I climbed back in gingerly. It was freezing now.

The next day dawned cold and crisp but bright and sunny and we loaded up the car. To be on the safe side, we checked the route with Richard and I packed some emergency food just in case. We followed the directions and headed directly to the coast road. From there we kept a sharp eye out for the turnoff to take us to Richard and Sarah's favourite beach which they'd said was stunning. As it was autumn, it wasn't swimming weather but a gorgeous day for a walk and some lunch at a lovely café on the beach. A roundabout appeared which had a sign on it for the exact beach we wanted, pointing down a road leading towards the coast. Easy, we thought.

So off we went. Once again we came to a couple of crossroads with no signage at all so logic prevailed and we chose to follow the one leading towards the coast. The road got narrower and bumpy; rows of grapevines appeared on either side of us. Then the road petered out and became a farm track and we began bouncing in and out of muddy potholes following tracks that looked like they'd been left by a tractor. We were by now jerking along parallel to two rows of grapevines heavy with bunches of red grapes so close I could've touched them.

We lurched into a particularly deep pothole and the bottom of the car made a loud, scraping noise.

'We're in a vineyard,' I said, stating the obvious.

'Where's the beach?' demanded the kids.

'Look at that big building up ahead. That must be a pretty big winery. I wonder if they do tastings or lunch?' I wondered.

'Well if not, there'll be somewhere to turn around at least,' replied Geoffrey, gripping the steering wheel tightly while trying to control the veering car.

'Oh, there's someone we can ask about wine tasting and get some directions to the beach,' I said as we pulled in at the large, ugly-looking winery. A man was standing out the front and looked rather dodgy. Maybe a farmworker, I thought. I wound the window down and leant out but Geoffrey suddenly floored it and took off.

'What the hell are you doing?' I shouted.

'It's a prison,' he yelled back. 'Wineries don't have four watchtowers complete with armed guards and a rim of barbed wire! I reckon that guy's just been released and is waiting for a lift; probably thought his luck was in there.'

I suppose the wine tasting's out then.

There was momentary silence while I processed this before laughing hard.

'This sucks,' said Jan. 'Why can't we do normal stuff on holiday? All we do is drive around all day lost. I want a coffee.'

Then Don chimed in. 'You promised us a beach and gave us a prison.'

'Well, we sort of mislaid the beach,' I replied.

'Yeah, like we sort of lose every place we try to get to.'

I couldn't argue with that one.

To cheer Don up, I said we would stop in Casoli at the supermarket and get some frozen wild boar tagliatelle. This appeased him slightly and a block of chocolate eased Jan's mood. When we finally got back to the house, Geoffrey had to go and find Richard to borrow some tools and together they reattached the part of the car's undercarriage that was hanging off from its trip to the seaside…ummm…prison.

Richard of course asked what we thought of the beach. Don took great delight in telling him that we hadn't been but went to a prison instead.

It wasn't until we returned home that I Googled the road we'd been on to see where we'd gone wrong and found out that we'd visited a high security prison for the very worst of the Italian Mafioso criminals.

THE DAGGER

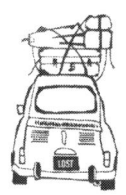

We headed to Rome to drop the car rental off on the outskirts. The city was on the list of banned places that Geoffrey wouldn't drive into and I couldn't blame him. Jan stayed on to do some further travelling while Geoffrey, Don and I started the long slog home to New Zealand. I'd said a tearful farewell to Jan and left Don to do his packing. Which was a mistake, as that boy isn't known for his common sense.

We flew from Rome to Dubai and arrived in the customs check area where our bags were X-rayed. To my utter horror, there on the screen, clearly visible to all the intimidating sheikhs, was the outline of a dagger in Don's carry-on luggage. Not a small dagger, but a huge one. *No, no, no, this cannot be happening.* It wasn't a good moment and it certainly got the sheikhs' attention. In my ignorance I was sure these guys were sheikhs. I'd never seen customs officers in full Arab robes before, so please bear with me. The one operating the X-ray machine stared transfixed at the screen for what seemed an eternity before calling his superiors over.

'Don,' I hissed, 'why the hell did you put a dagger in your carry-on bag? We're probably going to jail again now.'

'Well you told me to pack my bags and I did,' he muttered, looking sheepish and petrified all at once.

Another sheikh in long, white robes strode over and demanded to know whose bag it was.

'His.' We pointed at Don. Might as well save ourselves and try and get a good lawyer. Hopefully, he was underage and might be dealt with more leniently without the need to chop his head off or anything too drastic. This couldn't have happened in a worse country; you could be locked up for far lesser crimes there. Mind you, I was unable to think of any countries that would look too kindly on you taking a gigantic dagger onto an aircraft. *I couldn't possibly go to jail in Dubai; they don't drink alcohol. Imagine life without sauvignon blanc.*

Mr Sheikh ordered Don to hand over his passport and go with him. *Oh shit*, was all I could think. *We've done the Bosnian jail thing and now we're going to try a Dubai one.* Geoffrey headed off with Don but I couldn't follow as I was being pulled aside (again) because of the smallest of my four fans, the little battery-operated one in my handbag.

Only this was ever so slightly embarrassing as it was a man-fan which my friend had given me for my birthday. It was shaped like a man, only she'd glued on black woolly hair, a hairy chest and a little medallion to make it a Greek man-fan. *Oh gawd*, I thought, cringing and turning red as the sheikh held up man-fan for inspection. I couldn't think of any sensible explanation for having a fan in my bag dressed as a hairy Greek so decided to say nothing. He looked at me and shook his head then checked that it was indeed just a fan and established that I had issues with heat rather than explosives and I was free to go.

I joined the others and explained to Mr Sheikh that basically my son was an idiot, very much like his father who had allowed him to buy such a stupid thing in the first place, and we weren't aware there was a dagger in his bag and we were very, very, very sorry (yes, I grovelled shamelessly). Mr Sheikh glared at me then turned and, with a swish of his long, white robes, marched off to his computer and did some sheikh-type stuff on it.

'D'you think they wear undies under their robes?' I asked. No response from Geoffrey. We stood there shamefaced as our fellow passengers all filed through without any problem because apparently they didn't have concealed weapons in their bags. I felt like we were in the naughty corner, only with people who have the power to lock you up for an exceedingly long time.

After an eternity and a lot of typing, Mr Sheikh marched back over, barked that it was *'not* acceptable' and ordered Don to put the dagger in the seized-goods bin. He slapped Don's passport down on the desk with force, making us jump, and dismissed us with a definitive wave of his hand. We scuttled off, shamefaced. *Phew, thank goodness for that. I would be no good in a Dubai jail,* I thought. *I couldn't stand the heat and I doubt they have air con.*

When we arrived in Melbourne, Geoffrey declared the dagger which had been correctly packed, safely stowed in the checked-in luggage with a big sword Don had bought in Carcassonne (also while I wasn't present). Once again we were led away to be interviewed. The customs officer examined them both and decided the dagger was unacceptable and wasn't permitted to be brought into Australia even just to transit. So goodbye dagger and into the bin it went. The huge sword, however, was fine as it couldn't be deemed a concealable weapon. The officer looked at Geoffrey and me and shook his head. 'What's wrong with a souvenir T-shirt?' he asked.

'Don't include me in this,' I snapped. 'Put those two together and you would still have zero sense. Idiots.'

When we went through customs again to depart, my bag was put through the X-ray machine three times before they demanded to know who owned the bag. I shouted out that it was mine and I would be right there, just as soon as they'd finished swabbing me for drugs. You do have to wonder what their criteria is. Why did I look so suspicious? Perhaps they thought I had bulky packages taped under my clothes. No such luck. I'm afraid it was all natural. Once they'd established that my extra layers were in fact firmly attached to me and the swabs came back clear, I was free to go. I headed over to where the customs officer was searching my bag, expecting it to be Greek man-fan again.

But no, it was my tiny nail clippers this time, not even scissors, but blunt-edged clippers. The deadly items were seized in case I decided to take the pilot hostage and threaten to clip his toenails unless he took me to Cuba.

Upon returning home, we had more than photographs to remind us of our adventures. This time we also had bruises, sore necks and seatbelt haematomas.

Jan had a successful trip around Turkey and returned safely a few weeks later.

Don's sword hangs on his bedroom wall as a distinct reminder of what *not* to pack in your carry-on luggage.

2018

SOUTHEAST ASIA, MONTENEGRO, CROATIA, ITALY AND OMAN

THE CRUISE FROM HELL

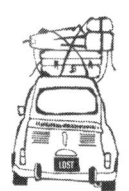

'Go on a cruise,' they said. 'It'll be fun,' they said. 'You'll love it,' they said. How could we resist? Our family of four boarded the ship in Singapore for an eleven-night cruise around Southeast Asia. I felt so excited as we boarded but after that it all went downhill pretty fast; well, from the moment we opened our cabin door.

We'd paid thousands for this cruise, sucked in by the advertised sale price, and as we thought we were getting a good deal we'd splashed out on a balcony room. It turned out to be the most expensive holiday of all time per length of the trip. The hidden extras had begun mounting up well before sailing, to the point that we were over the cruise before we were on it.

So after all the expense, we opened our cabin door with great expectations, only to find we were going to be living in a cramped shoe box. But the main issue was there were four of us and only three beds—two singles with a fold-down bunk above one of them yet we'd booked a quad room, which you would assume had space to accommodate four people. There wasn't even a couch for the fourth person to perch on.

This mystery was solved later when we returned from dinner to find a trundle bed-cum-stretcher had been set up in the room by the housekeeper. We stood and stared. After we'd shelled out mega bucks for the pleasure of having a balcony, that was now out of bounds, so were the fridge, the dresser and pretty much any walking area apart from the entrance. Don's bed was now wedged diagonally across the space between the balcony and the single bed. To fit it in, the housekeeper had had to move the small table and a chair and these were now blocking the end of a single bed so you couldn't walk around it. To get across, you had to roll over that bed, climb onto the trundle bed (difficult when someone was asleep in either) and pull yourself up to squeeze onto the balcony. We were dumbfounded. Geoffrey and Don were already on the cruise under duress and this wasn't helping.

Over the following days, we enjoyed the scintillating activities on offer such as veggie- and fruit-sculpting, ice-carving demonstrations, diamond jewellery sales and champagne art auctions interspersed with gatherings for the elite club members. Geoffrey and Don sulked in the cabin, refusing to come out. They would've sulked on the deck sunbathing and swimming except it was raining and the wind was howling.

Things at sea were pretty posh. We were not. There was a ridiculously high standard of formal dress required just for the right to eat dinner in the dining room. Dress shorts, belt, shirt and even a bow tie weren't good enough for a seventeen-year-old young man. Don had to have long, formal trousers so we were evicted.

We were forced to listen to posh people who, with loud voices, tried to outdo each other on the number of cruises they'd been on, their VIP loyalty status and who had dined with the captain. And then there was the buffet where these same people barked orders at staff, treating them with disdain and a sense of entitlement.

After two days of these pleasures at sea, we arrived at our first port of Borneo and at last we could get off. But it wasn't that simple. You see, what we needed first was to be trained in the art of herding. We duly wore our colour-coded stickers on our tops and gathered with our fellow, colour-coded passengers, awaiting our leader with the magic paddle held aloft so we could follow them like mindless morons.

Well, that was fun wasn't it? Oh but wait, there's more. Due to a typhoon in the South China Sea, we were stuck there for another day as the ocean was too rough to cross to Vietnam. Everyone sat on the boat sighing and moaning a bit more as they crisped their leathery old skin up in the sun, which had finally emerged, and drank expensive cocktails. The cruise-ship company had long since drained our bank account dry so we drank the free drinks from the dispensers: water or iced tea.

After two days at dock in Borneo, the captain had a surge of bravado and decided it couldn't be that bad. It was just a typhoon so bon voyage and we set sail across the wide, open South China Sea into the tail end of a typhoon; just swells of nine to eleven metres, nothing to worry about. We didn't hear another word from the good ole captain for the next two days as we were tossed around the ocean. The onboard shop sold out of seasickness tablets and we lay on our beds, gripping the sides during the day to stop from being tossed onto the floor. At night when I couldn't see the sea, I contemplated wearing my lifejacket to bed.

We mightn't have been able to see the waves but we could certainly hear them coming, smashing into the bow of the ship then shuddering and jolting down the entire length of the boat. The noise, along with the groaning and howling wind, was terrifying. To move around the cabin, we were forced to brace against the wall and stagger. There was no entertainment on deck in the howling gale unless you counted watching the tsunami waves washing back and forth in the pools. Finally after two days and nights of this, we arrived to the calm waters of Ho Chi Minh, Vietnam, having missed the port of Nha Trang.

We elected to have free time there, using the cruise-ship bus to ride into the city then meeting it back at the same spot—the Bitexco Financial Tower—at 3 p.m. After a brief wander around the war museum, Jan and I left the boys to catch a cab to China Town to look at authentic, old-town Vietnam. I had the address printed on a piece of paper for the taxi driver and it was in English and Vietnamese to avoid any confusion. There was a taxi stand in front of the museum so it appeared that they must be official taxis. Being reasonably savvy, I asked the driver to turn on the meter, not wanting to be hit with an exorbitant cost when we arrived.

From the map in my hand, China Town would appear to be only five to eight kilometres away so shouldn't have taken long. However, we drove for ages and all the while the meter clicked away rapidly. Jan and I exchanged looks and a feeling of unease settled in.

Eventually we stopped in the middle of a vast, busy, run-down area with no sign of China Town. I heard the car door locks click and the driver leant over, all pleasantries gone, and demanded 650,000 Vietnamese dong for a journey that should have cost around 80,000. I gave him what I had, everything in my purse, and said, 'That's it,' and attempted to get out but the doors were still locked. Jan tried her door and found it was also locked. 'No more money,' I said.

'Give me all your money,' he barked. 'She has; she has. I see it. Give me,' he angrily shouted, looking at Jan and snapping his fingers together with impatience. He forced her to open her purse and snatched all the notes she had, released the door locks and said calmly, 'Not safe, ladies, hang onto purse!'

Are you serious? Unbelievable.

We stepped out, thankful to be free of that hateful man as he sped off. We took stock of our surroundings and our situation then tried our phones but they didn't work as we were in another country without a local SIM card. We didn't have any cash to catch a bus or taxi. There wasn't much time until the cruise-ship bus departed and we had no way of contacting anyone for help. *Shit, shit, shit.* As I looked around us, everything was alien. Cockerels in wire cages pecked at the grass around us. We were on the median strip of an insanely busy, four-lane road, full of chaotic rickshaws, scooters and cars; both sides of the road were lined with a shanty town of colourful but rickety shops, lean-tos and stalls selling anything from lanterns to herbal remedies. Everyone was staring at us. Well, I got authentic!

We formed a plan to look for an ATM or a bank to get some cash then try to catch another cab back to the pickup point. This plan was soon dashed when we found a bank then discovered it was closed as was the next one as it was Sunday. We located an ATM but it wouldn't accept our cards. Next we came across a little hostel and asked inside for help but they couldn't understand English. Everyone we attempted to speak to either ignored us, walked away or spoke no English.

We were up shit creek without a paddle, as the saying goes. Hot, sweaty and tired. It was about 35 degrees; we only had a little water with us and no money to purchase drinks or lunch. The Vietnamese stared at us with suspicion. I felt unwelcome and unsafe but perhaps this was due to our predicament. We were feeling desperate now and trying not to panic as there had been no sign of other tourists. We were alone and it was time for a miracle. In my mind I saw that cruise ship sailing away, with Geoffrey and Don left wondering whatever became of us.

Suddenly in the distance and heading our way, I saw two European-looking ladies followed by a group. I dashed towards them, desperation written across my face as I gibbered out our predicament. They were a party of Germans with a local tour guide, exploring the area. The woman explained what I said to the tour guide and told us we could go with them. Their English wasn't that good either, but we followed them along the pavement, unsure what would happen next. Suddenly a bus appeared and the tour guide motioned us on board, cleared two seats for us up the front and told us they would drop us at the Notre-Dame Cathedral near where we needed to be.

As we climbed aboard, we finally breathed and I felt so relieved I could've cried. We should just have enough time to dash from the Notre-Dame to our pickup point. As we sat back and relaxed a little, the tour guide stood at the front of the bus and explained to the rest of the Germans that these two nit-wits were scammed and robbed by a taxi driver and dumped near where they found us.

'No taxis in Ho Chi Minh,' he said gravely, shaking his head. 'No, no, no.'

As I sat back, gazing out of the window, I listened to the commentary in German and the humorous side of our sorry tale dawned on me and I chuckled to myself. We went to see China Town, got abducted, robbed and dumped and now here we were cruising around the sights of Ho Chi Minh with front row seats on a luxury tour bus full of Germans. No one would believe us when we got back to the ship.

After we thanked the tour guide at the cathedral, he dragged us across the four-way intersection, stood us facing down a long, straight avenue and said, 'Walk, stay on this street; maybe two kilometres then you come to your bus.' So off we went. I was so hot, tired and thirsty, but needs must; heads down we marched as fast as our legs would go and didn't stop. We got to the meeting point with fifteen minutes to spare and returned safely to the ship.

Next day we docked in Sihanoukville, Cambodia. After a quick game of colour-coded herding, the ship's buses dropped the passengers off outside the local market where the melee of hopeful personal tour guides were waiting in a mob to pounce. Many of the posh people around us were horrified and refused to get off the bus. They returned straight back to the sterile safety of the ship. We, on the other hand, couldn't wait to escape. Our family spent one of the most memorable days together in this impoverished region of Cambodia, humbled by the warmth and generosity of the people. This turned out to be the one highlight of this miserable holiday. Our guide, Mr Rony, was the most gracious of hosts and we parted company at the end of the day with a warmth normally reserved for familiar friends.

Later in the evening, we set sail for Bangkok, Thailand. We again booked the cruise-ship bus to take us into the city for free time to sightsee before pickup hour. The advertised one-and-a-half-hour bus ride each way was three hours, leaving the frustrated passengers just three hours to explore Bangkok.

Map in hand and a list of attractions to see, we were ready to explore. Oh but wait, what's that, you say? The tour guide informed us they wouldn't be dropping us anywhere near the actual city or any attractions. They would drop us at a suburban mall. What, you want to see Bangkok? Not possible. It would take two hours to get to central Bangkok. Enjoy the mall. I later found out that parking for buses in the city centre costs the cruise-ship companies more so it was far cheaper for them just to dump us at a mall.

We had mutiny on the bus and we got off with thunderous faces, went to a mall, ate lunch in the food court and headed back to the bus. After a head count, we realised two women were missing. So we waited while the tour guide rang the ship to let them know we would be delayed. After what had happened to Jan and me, I was worried about them; not so the nobs we were with. After twenty minutes they started yelling at the Thai tour guide to leave them behind or they would be late for the buffet. The poor woman rang the ship again and said we would be waiting another 30 minutes. We were horrified when our fellow passengers started chanting, 'Leave them, leave them,' while stamping their feet.

Thankfully the two missing women came puffing and panting up to the bus, climbed on and burst into tears, apologising profusely. They too had been driven off into the middle of nowhere and been forced to hand all their money to the driver. It was just lucky they'd been rescued by a truck driver and brought back to the bus. Sound familiar? As we talked among the group, we found out two of the others had been abducted by a taxi in Ho Chi Minh and dumped on the docks miles from the ship.

ONE WAY

The morning of our Koh Samui visit dawned a beautiful day. I know this because while Don was in the toilet retching violently, I took the rare opportunity to clamber across his empty stretcher bed to gain access to the balcony. Poor Don had come down with the dreaded cruise-ship squits.

Hence only three of us got off the ship, leaving him to rest. He had room service for anything he needed and the housekeeper to check on him. I should add that he was a young adult by this point, not a child being abandoned. Koh Samui was stunning but our time all too short as we didn't want to leave Don for too long. Back on board we took him down to the bowels of the ship (excuse the pun) to see the ship's doctor who confirmed Norovirus, supplied Don with a full array of drugs and confined him to our cabin. He was under house arrest and not to go out in public areas.

We were now at sea, heading south through the Gulf of Thailand back towards Singapore. The next morning Geoffrey woke up feeling sick. Seriously, did a big, dark genie of doom just follow our family around, tapping us with a giant wand of shit? At this stage I didn't even know why I was surprised. So two down, Jan and I did the only sensible thing: bathed ourselves in sanitiser and went for coffee. The ship was due to dock the next day and our flights were booked for that night. Would the two patients be fit to fly? Geoffrey headed down to visit the ship's doctor and was also placed under house arrest with enough drugs to dope a hippo.

Later there was a knock at our cabin door and there stood a swat team of masked men in white boiler suits. We sat feeling uncomfortable as they thoroughly swabbed down our bathroom. It felt like our toilet was the scene of some heinous crime. Food was left on trays at our door; other passengers in the corridor gave us a wide berth; they might as well have painted a black cross on the door. Jan and I just sighed. We rang our travel insurance to check we were covered if medically unable to fly. The doctor called our room later in the day to say we were to stay there the next morning and we would be medically disembarked separately to all the other passengers.

The following day, Don was a little better but Geoffrey was feeling worse, feverish but not vomiting. We were escorted off the ship by the boiler-suit brigade and shoved in a taxi for the airport. We said goodbye to Jan, who was joining a friend and heading off on a group tour around Thailand; she was flying to Bangkok the next day.

We cancelled all our plans for a day out sightseeing around Singapore. While the patients dozed and dribbled, I had plenty of time to reflect on just what a splendid holiday it had been. But it was a holiday that just kept on giving, as we were about to find out.

When we arrived home, the phone rang. Jan was in Bangkok International Hospital with severe food poisoning; of course she was. Not only that, but it had struck while she was at the airport departure gate, leaving her standing in the gate lounge, vomiting into the rubbish bin. Oh the humiliation. But the bad luck genie hadn't finished with us yet.

Geoffrey's Norovirus didn't go away. Three expensive visits to the doctor later, it was confirmed he had Avian Influenza type-A. I looked up at the genie of doom and silently said, 'Don't you dare.'

He ignored me and I got it too.

A DOSE OF SMALLPOX

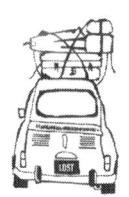

Later that year, with our adult children busy leading their own lives—Jan working on a cruise ship in the Caribbean and Don at university—Geoffrey and I set off as empty nesters on new adventures. Not surprisingly we chose to go with a different car rental company for this trip, hiring a Citroën we nicknamed Cedric. And where did Geoffrey request we return to? Surprise, surprise—Venice.

We began our seven-week journey with a few days exploring parts of the city we hadn't yet seen, beginning with the early morning market where local Venetians shop daily; Teatro la Fenice, a famous opera house; the Jewish ghetto and Ca' Rezzonico, a magnificent palace on the Grand Canal. It was hot, humid and thirsty work.

Fully satiated with culture, we stopped at a sidewalk restaurant for a late lunch and were shown to a table by the waiter, who seemed quite surprised when I greeted him with the French *bonjour* rather than the Italian *buongiorno*. He returned a few moments later with a complimentary basket of bread and asked if we wanted to order some drinks.

I carefully asked in my bestest Italian for a bottle of fizzy water. '*Una bottiglia d'acqua gazole.*'

Geoffrey gasped; the waiter spluttered; this was too much!

'Why you keep talking French to me? You are notta French, and you in Italia?' the waiter asked with great drama. 'Now you order a bottle of fizzy petrol to drink?' He stomped inside, waving his arms about.

A few moments later, laughter erupted from within and another waiter popped his head out to see the crazy lady. Geoffrey was doubled over. I was confused.

'What did I say that was wrong?' I asked.

'*Gazole* is French for petrol or diesel. You were meant to say *gassata* for fizzy.' He roared, unable to stop laughing.

Oh shit. It might be time to leave Venice.

After one more day exploring the nearby Burano Island, we headed down the Dalmatian coast of Croatia to Kotor in Montenegro for a week to stay in a holiday rental apartment overlooking the Bay of Kotor.

We managed to leave Montenegro with Cedric's undercarriage still intact after a foray into the bay. Geoffrey's top driving tips for the stupid among us now include how *not* to reverse into the Bay of Kotor. Let me briefly bring you up to speed.

As we drove along the edge of the water on a dazzlingly sunny, warm day, we decided to stop at a small bar by the water for a drink. Geoffrey drove past two empty car parks for reasons known only to himself so then had to reverse back into a parking space. There was a little parking bay jutting out over the water which ended with a stone wall dropping to a narrow stretch of sand and water below.

Geoffrey began reversing but suddenly the back of the car on my side dropped away with a thud.

'Shit! What's that?' I shouted.

'Just a pothole,' replied Geoffrey with blind confidence as he carried on reversing. With that, his rear tyre plunged over the stone wall and we were left dangling on the edge. Geoffrey shouted, 'F#@%,' pulled on the handbrake to stop us plunging over and then slammed the car into first, gunning the engine. I was screaming and trying to bail out before we landed in the bay. The engines screamed; tyres squealed and a smell of burning rubber filled the air.

Finally we gained traction and landed back on terra firma.

I stared at Geoffrey open-mouthed, heart beating rapidly. 'You're a complete dick. You know I can't swim.'

We clambered out to inspect Cedric's nether regions only to find a poor Russian woman looking pale and shocked beneath us, innocently trying to sunbathe until a Citroën had nearly landed on her head. We couldn't converse so shrugged and looked sheepish. She laughed. I looked up.

'Oh God,' I groaned. All eyes were upon us, with everyone in the bar staring and locals hanging out of windows, open-mouthed. I wanted to get straight back in the car and head out of there as it was so embarrassing but Geoffrey said no, he'd successfully found a car park and we were staying.

Having survived the rest of our week in Montenegro, we drove to Split to take the car ferry to the Croatian island of Korčula where we stayed in a private holiday cottage owned by a lady called Dina. The apartment was just outside Korčula old town and overlooked the Adriatic Sea.

I was happy to be sitting later on the terrace of our accommodation with a cuppa, enjoying the sea breeze and a view of the Adriatic while listening carefully for any rustling sounds in the garden that might indicate the presence of Dina's free-ranging tortoises. We were only a short walk from Korčula Stari Grad, or Old Town, the birthplace of Marco Polo. Cedric was safely stowed away in a garage for a few days so I was free from Geoffrey's driving incidents.

'Where's Geoffrey?' you ask. One of his teeth had been playing up since Montenegro where he refused to go to the dentist and do something about it. The pain had now worsened so Geoffrey had gone to lie on his death bed while I Googled a dentist. Dr Kastalan seemed to have all the pre-requisites required: he appeared to be a human and it said he was a dentist; nothing but the best for our Geoffrey. Hopefully he spoke English.

After a restless night of pain, Geoffrey was up and off on foot to search for the dentist at 8 a.m. What he found was the hospital where he was told to go upstairs and wait. There were three doors, each containing a dentist, but no reception so he poked his head through one door and found Dr Kastalan. He spoke reasonable English and sent Geoffrey off around the hospital with a piece of paper to have an X-ray and a full 360-degree scan of his head which cost a grand total of 60 kuna ($9). Then he trotted back to Dr Kastalan who apologised for keeping Geoffrey waiting for two minutes. He already had the X-rays displayed on his screen which confirmed he needed a root canal. Then just like that, the dentist drilled the tooth without pain relief (ouch), cleaned it out, filled it with antibiotic paste and capped it off. A grand total of 150 kuna ($22.50). Dr Kastalan told Geoffrey that many overseas patients came to have dental work done, including many Kiwis and Aussies who combined it with their European holiday. Who'd have thought it? Clearly my thorough research into finding Geoffrey the best dentist had paid off.

By now I was up so had achieved all I wanted out of my day (only kidding). I was poking around the garden still searching for the elusive tortoises. I didn't find one but discovered Stuart. He heard me and realised a new lot of suckers had arrived at the house. I fed him Geoffrey's salami. Oh yeah, and Stuart's a cat.

Once Geoffrey returned he was formally introduced to Stuart before we strolled into the fortified old town of Korčula located on a raised knoll. We walked around its perimeter walls before finding the Marco Polo Museum. On the way out, I finally spotted what I'd been searching for: giant, inflatable floaties. I selected my floatie of choice— a giant pineapple—and left feeling complete. Now that we were fully knowledgeable on Marco Polo and proud owners of a giant, and very heavy, plastic pineapple, we headed to Konzum supermarket. We stuffed what we could carry in our cloth bags, trudging home in the heat. Beaded in sweat I eagerly anticipated a cool dip in the ocean.

While I put the groceries away, the sky went dark, then, bang, wind was suddenly howling; the temperature dropped about twenty degrees and the beach turned into a white-water frenzy. Boats zoomed for shore in the gale-force winds; beachgoers grabbed their belongings and scattered. My pineapple and I sat miserably looking out of the window. Geoffrey had gone to bed for a siesta; even Stuart had disappeared. Oh, but wait. What was that sound? I looked up from the couch. Alarmingly I heard our front door open then American voices. The door opened and in strolled two tourists bold as brass into my flipping lounge and asked to book a room. I don't know who was more startled—them or me. As they looked around, it finally dawned on them that they weren't in reception but in my lounge. They slunk out apologetically and I slammed and bolted the door behind them.

Due to the storm, most of the eateries along the seafront were closed so we found ourselves in an interesting little café drinking free shots of fiery raki provided by the owner in recognition of Geoffrey's linguistic skills. He'd just been praised for his pronunciation of the local language. It didn't matter what country we were in, Geoffrey often now picked up the language just like that. It was infuriating. As I perused the menu, something caught my eye. I did a double take but no, it wasn't my eyesight. Listed on the menu was a plate of smallpox. Oooh, now that was appealing. I had to order it just for the opportunity to ask for a plate of smallpox. The waiter didn't even flinch but commented that it was a good choice. I waited with anticipation for my dish to arrive and, voilà, my disease-ridden main was revealed to be shrimp risotto, very tasty too for a noxious disease.

After the main, Geoffrey asked for the dessert menu.

'No, we need to go now,' I hissed.

'Why? I want dessert,' grumbled Geoffrey.

'Stuart must have fleas,' I muttered. 'My ankles are so itchy, I'm going to scream.'

We fled the restaurant and I spent the night twisting about, convulsed with frenzied scratching. Next day Stuart and I were no longer friends. Perhaps that was karma for feeding him Geoffrey's salami.

I was now looking forward to getting off this island. Between teeth, storms, strangers in my lounge and fleas, I was over it. I was woken by Geoffrey's cell phone ringing, followed by his dulcet tones shouting, 'Well that's just typical, isn't it?'

I climbed out of bed, noting the lumpy, red, swollen bites decorating my legs and asked, 'What's happening?'

'That was Dina. The storms sparked a forest fire raging out of control on the mainland right down to the road. All ferries are cancelled. We're stuck here.'

ABRUZZO MAGIC

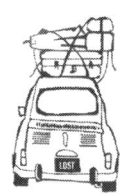

We finally succeeded in leaving Korčula for Split where we boarded the good ship *Marco Polo* once again, the overnight ferry that would take us to Ancona on the eastern coast of Italy. Only this time there were thankfully just the two of us boarding and we hadn't managed to kill Cedric so were able to drive on and leave most of the luggage in the car.

We'd been lured back to the Abruzzo by the warm friendliness of the people and the untouched, wild landscapes. It was pure, unedited Italian life that offered us history and nature without the crowds.

Rocca Calascio is a mountaintop fortress in the Province of L'Aquila in the Abruzzo. At an elevation of 1,460 metres, it's the highest fortress in the Apennines, dating back to the 10th century. It's surrounded by the Gran Sasso National Park where bears and wolves still roam and the Maremma Sheepdogs watch over sheep. We'd arrived to stay in the medieval stone village nestled against the rocky outcrop just below the castle. Rifugio della Rocca is a family-run cooperative where the family are gradually restoring the village houses into accommodation, with the restaurant, bar, café and concert hall taking centre stage.

Paulo warmly greeted us after we'd dragged our suitcases up from the car park below, across ancient and worn cobblestones. We followed him up to the original, renovated stone house, ducking to enter the old, arched doorway after he'd inserted a key of ginormous proportions. The accommodation was simply stunning; we felt like we'd stepped back in time and shared a glimpse into what it might have been like to live within these walls. The room was authentically renovated, keeping as many original features as possible: age-old, terracotta floor tiles, stone arches and lintels, the fireplace complete with centuries of blackened smoke staining the stone surround, and ancient shutters. The furnishings were antiques sympathetic to the era of the house.

It was cool at this elevation and a foggy mist descended around us. We were surrounded by stone ruins, village houses awaiting their turn to be restored to life. I went to draw in the shutters across the door as Geoffrey lit a fire in the ancient fireplace. Before I could shut the door, a little black and white cat sauntered in, meowed, leapt on the bed and settled in, purring while awaiting attention. I named him Raphael, our Italian cat. Hopefully this one didn't have fleas. Geoffrey and I shared a glass of the local Montepulciano d'Abruzzo red wine before exploring the village further, accompanied by Raphael.

That night, as we were the only guests, Paulo asked if we were happy for his brother Pietro to prepare for us a selection of seasonal dishes using local ingredients. We readily agreed. The region specialises in traditional fare such as shepherd's stew, rabbit and wild boar dishes. Later we were joined by a further overnight guest, Roberto, a landscape photographer from Rome who was there on assignment to capture the castle's beauty using time-lapse photography. We couldn't converse with him as he didn't speak English but Paulo acted briefly as a translator to make introductions before returning to the kitchen.

We sat next to an ancient and smoke-blackened fireplace. Through the little shuttered window, we could see a few sparse lights twinkling far below us in the valley. Mama arrived and joined her boys in the kitchen. There was much chatter; the room filled with rich aromas while the fire crackled and another cat wandered in to seek the warmth of the fire. Fully satiated after a dinner of Abruzzo-style barley broth, traditional ravioli with tomato and local pecorino cheese, followed by shepherd's stew of lamb and potatoes, Geoffrey and I stepped out into the crisp, cool mountain air for a short walk up to our historic village house. The old street lamps cast a ghostly glow in the mist. I shivered, imagining the centuries of life and energy absorbed into these stones, imagining what they'd seen and what they could tell us.

I awoke early and, peering through the shutters, I spied Raphael waiting patiently on the doorstep. I turned the heavy iron key then pushed open the old, wooden shutters to peep out into the morning fog clinging to the high peaks surrounding us. To my utter astonishment, I found Raphael had brought his friend Signore Fox, who was sitting waiting a few feet away from our door. I grabbed my phone and some digestive biscuits (for lack of immediate fox-type food), whispered at Geoffrey to come quickly as there was a fox, then slipped out of the door.

Signore Fox took a digestive biscuit that I tossed him and headed off into the village, munching as he went with me and Raphael and now Geoffrey in hot pursuit. We caught up with the fox outside the restaurant where the owner was giving him leftover bread. Signore Fox ran off and Geoffrey watched him burying it for later in a spot behind a ruin. The owner explained that during summer when food is plentiful, they don't see the fox, then he starts coming in late autumn and over winter when needing to store or supplement his supplies. He arrived early in the morning as the sun rose and waited for the owner to chuck out the bread, vanishing again before the first wave of daily walkers entered the village. We felt very special to have witnessed Signore Fox's appearance and to be able to feed him and admire his amazing, reddish fur coat and brilliantly thick, luxurious tail.

During a hearty breakfast provided by Mama, we watched the furls of mist lift, revealing the layers of hills and valleys rippling below us.

The fire crackled, dispelling the chill air, and yet more cats sauntered in. Stomachs bulging, we set off up the track leading to Chiesa di Santa Maria della Pietà, an unusual, octagonal-shaped church built in 1596 during the Renaissance period. Sadly this beautiful building standing on a promontory overlooking the valley was damaged by an earthquake in the 18th century. As we walked up to the church, we spotted two foxes gambolling around in a meadow far below us. The wildflowers growing in abundance around us were magnificent: pink and purple varieties of alpine veronica, valerian, forget-me-not and scabious.

It was so peaceful with just the sound of our footsteps crunching on the gravel. Towering above us were the defensive outer walls of the Rocca Calascio Castle, the highest fortress in the Apennines, offering us occasional glimpses of the mighty castle within.

A little way further past the church, we climbed over large, rough rocks, some lying where they'd fallen, damaged over the centuries by earthquakes. A metal and wooden keep offered access to enter the castle across a defensive ditch. Inside we entered the turrets. As we peered through the arrow slits, it was as if we could see forever. It was easy to see why 1,000 years ago this spot was chosen to build a defensive fort. There was no one around except for us and Roberto, who greeted us warmly before returning to his tripod. What a privilege it was to be up there, feeling like we were on top of the world and having it all to ourselves without any sign of human habitation.

We wandered about and found a spot to sit and enjoy the view and the peace while munching on our bag of dried figs from Hvar in Croatia. We were gazing out at high altitude grasslands, tussock grasses interspersed with colourful wildflowers while rising behind were the snow-draped mountain peaks of the Grand Sasso National Park. Snaking remnants of long-ago rock walls and stone shelters broke up the landscape. Then, perfecto, I brought out the Kit Kats. Other day-walkers started arriving as we got back to the bottom. After a restorative coffee in the bar, we retired for a quick siesta in our tower house before heading down to the restaurant for a lunch of some wild boar ragu with homemade pasta.

Paulo got out his phone and offered a suggestion for the afternoon, which was a loop road along the Campo Imperatore, an alpine plateau 1,500 metres high in the Apennine Ridge, known as little Tibet. After lunch we set off. What a superb recommendation; the area was magnificent. It felt a world away from the Italy that most tourists experience as Cedric the Citroën ably took us through a high, grassy plateau filled with wildflowers and surrounded by snow-covered, jagged peaks. Herds of slowly munching cows meandered about freely with their bells clanging with their movements. This melodic sound echoed around the basin.

For hundreds of years, shepherds in the Abruzzo have moved their flocks of sheep south in the autumn to lower pastures following pre-Roman routes before winter comes. Maremmano-Abruzzese Sheepdogs help them, a traditional movement of sheep and cows called the transhumance. Shepherds go with each flock and carry a bed roll and supplies, camping with the herd and guarding them with the trusty and watchful eyes of the sheepdogs to protect against attack by wolves or foxes. The shepherds could use trucks to move their stock but the Abruzzo people hold dear their traditions.

As luck would have it, Geoffrey and I visited during the very week that the shepherds, sheepdogs and the herds of sheep and cows (complete with bells) were moving across the Campo Imperatore and down to lower pastures. It was a great surprise to round a corner and come across two of these enormous white dogs standing imposingly by the side of the road; we briefly thought they were wolves as they had such long legs.

When we returned to Rifugio della Rocca, we parked the car at the top of the switchback road that led almost to the top of the mountain then continued on foot up into the long-ago abandoned village. It was filled with the sound of workmen busy restoring the next house to liveable order. Many of the buildings were further damaged in the 2009 L'Aquila earthquake and had been stabilised with metal rods until it was their turn for restoration. We imagined what it would be like a few years from then. We learned that the family held concerts and festivals there in the summer with more and more overseas visitors being drawn by the magical qualities of the Abruzzo region. Artisans were setting up businesses in some of the village houses, trying to create a genuine village that could once again support a small population.

As we sat tucked up by the fire, Raphael on the bed in our ancient tower house, we reflected on what an exceptional place this was; somewhere we wouldn't forget in a hurry. The fact that we got to enjoy Signore Fox and the castle in splendid solitude gave us a selfish sense of satisfaction as we watched the day-visitors tramping back down past our door. They looked up with surprise and more than a little envy when they saw me looking out of the small wooden shutters of my personal stone tower. Our stomachs were preparing for whatever Pietro was cooking for us for dinner. This time a barley broth was followed by three-cheese gnocchi with roasted rabbit legs, which were delicious, cooked in a local Abruzzo red wine.

Signore Fox was outside again early the following day. Satisfied with his oat cookie, he headed down to the restaurant to see what Pietro had on offer, after which he ate out of Geoffrey's hand. How special was that? After Mama's breakfast we headed into a nearby village to explore and brought Raphael some cat food before returning to the Campo Imperatore plateau. Here we dined outdoors Abruzzese style on traditional shepherd's food of lamb skewered on sticks and cooked over a BBQ. Long, thin, metal troughs called canala, shaped like a gutter, were filled with hot charcoal ready for the arrosticini skewers of lamb to rest across. Laden with our arrosticini and sausages, we chose a grill and cooked our lunch, a convivial way of dining, sharing grills and conversation while cooking alongside each other. The lamb was divine.

As we drove on, we came across a herd of free-ranging horses across the road, snoozing and munching grass beside it; they were relaxed and unfazed by our presence. A couple of tourists approached them and lay down in the grass with a foal. After roaming among the horses, we carried on a short distance before coming to the huge cows also freely wandering all over the road with their giant bells melodically clanging, then past a shepherd watching his flock. Positioned around the hills flanking the valley were the Maremmano-Abruzzese Sheepdogs keeping watch for wolves. A little further on we got out to admire the mountains and one of the huge sheepdogs came ambling over; two others were watching from the hill above. He was awfully skinny so I got out a tin of Raphael's cat food and Geoffrey tipped it out for him. It was gone in one gulp so I gave him our other can. *Sorry, Raphael, no dinner for you tonight.* The dog was beautiful and let us pat him.

Pressing onward we eventually found the most perfect spot to stop and sit gazing at the sheer, jagged, snow-covered peak of the Corno Grande ahead of us while we ate our nectarines and figs. I've never eaten a more delicious nectarine, made all the more tasty by the stunning scenery surrounding us and the pure, blissful silence, punctuated by the occasional clanging of cow bells.

We arrived back at our tower house to see Paulo and Roberto unlocking the restored building opposite our tower which acted as a concert hall. They beckoned for us to come in. After we'd climbed the heavy, worn stone steps, we entered the room where a grand piano sat atop a small wooden stage at the far end, backlit by the light streaming in the little window behind the piano. The room was small with a few rows of wooden bench seats for the audience. The ceiling was a masterpiece of finely crafted and restored timbers in all their arched glory.

This was the room where the musically talented family held classical concerts once a month. It wasn't a scheduled performance but Roberto had asked to include this experience in the article he was writing to go with his photographs. Mama and some elderly family members arrived. We took a seat and Paulo sat down at the grand piano and proceeded to produce music that was so beautifully emotive it made the hairs on the back of my neck stand up.

When he finished there was a chorus of 'bravo, bravo' and applause. A few day-trippers timidly poked their heads through the doorway to see what was happening, before retreating. Once again we had the feeling of being so privileged to be here on the inside, gaining this insight into the lives of the locals. Paulo continued graciously to play a few tunes before dragging Mama up with him to do a splendid duet. It was lovely to see them play together and to witness the warmth of their mother-son relationship. At the conclusion of the unexpected and delightful concert, they turned the iron key and the village again fell silent. This place had been full of surprises.

We were sad to leave the Abruzzo with a farewell to Raphael who sat and meowed next to our suitcases. Mama sent us on our way with some homemade cakes as she was worried lest we got hungry on the long journey down to Puglia in the south. She remained suspicious about the quality of their food; best to stock up on good Abruzzo fare.

Tutto bene. All was well.

FAULTY TOWERS TROPEA

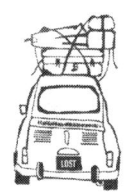

In Puglia we stayed in one of the traditional trulli houses—circular, limestone homes with a conical-shaped, tiled roof. We were there principally to see Matera, a complex of cave dwellings carved into the ancient river canyon, and the traditional villages of trulli houses around Alberobello in the Itria Valley. The weather wasn't kind to us that week so my main impression was that trulli are small with very thick stone walls which seemed to hold a lot of moisture. I spent a long time blow-drying socks, bras and undies with a hair dryer. Our trullo was one circular room with a bathroom attached; there was nowhere for Geoffrey and I to escape from each other. It was time to head towards Sicily.

We pulled up into the hotel carpark at the base of a cliff. We congratulated ourselves on successfully locating Tropea, a small town on the east coast of Calabria, without incident. We were just there for one night on our way to Sicily, and Cedric the Citroën and Sassy the antagonistic satnav had both behaved themselves. Having arrived at the most stunning location with blue skies, sparkling seas and white sand after a long drive, we were eager to check in and hit the beach. It was a fine day indeed when everything went right.

There was no one in reception. We waited as there was no bell. I re-read my paperwork. Jenny, the only English speaker at the hotel, was supposed to meet us there but seemed to have gone AWOL. We stepped outside the reception office and tried to attract the attention of a staff member but they all seemed to be scurrying around, setting up for a magnificent Italian christening party on the terrace and studiously ignored us.

Nonna, who was sitting nodding off in the sun, shuffled over and rattled off some rapid-fire Italian at us. The fact that we couldn't speak Italian was no deterrent for her. She continued with the fast talk then grasped that we were stupid, shrugged and walked off. *Oh for gawd's sake. What the hell sort of place is this*? It was fast going from hotel to *Hi-de-Hi!*[1] holiday camp.

But Nonna was no quitter. She returned, grasped my arm and dragged me with her while she shuffled around the place, yelling with ear-piercing shrieks for the missing Jenny, who remained steadfastly missing. Hope fading, Nonna changed tack and tugged me along as she approached all the staff, asking them in Italian if they could speak English and tell the ding-a-lings what was happening. All sources exhausted, poor Nonna flopped down on a deckchair; we did likewise. What else was there to do? Geoffrey and I looked at each other.

'I knew it was too bloody good to be true,' he grumbled.

All we could do was gaze longingly at the sea and wait in the heat. Nonna sat up. She had a lightbulb moment, pulled a cell phone out of her apron pocket, rang Jenny and screamed at her. We waited. Jenny got there pronto to check us in.

She wanted cash. I raised my eyebrows as Mafia money-laundering ran through my mind. I told her we had no cash and insisted on paying with a credit card. Jenny sighed heavily like I was bringing her much pain and aggravation before informing us that we couldn't eat at the hotel as it was her granddaughter's christening. It was our turn to sigh. Great, we would have to go out again. But wait, all was not lost. We were entitled to a complimentary welcome drink on the terrace once we'd taken our bags up to our room. So we popped down to the bar for a refreshing drink before having a swim. We sat; we waited; there was no barman; there was no bell.

After a long, dry wait, we gave up. The sea was calling us for a swim. But first Geoffrey had to inflate the pineapple. He wasn't too happy about this, given its size. Eventually we strutted down to the beach past all the bathers. Geoffrey walked into the water first. Down the steep, stony beach, two steps in and he fell over, knocked off his feet and onto his butt by a big swell. The sunbathers looked up, sensing entertainment. They weren't disappointed.

Inside the pineapple I strutted more cautiously down into the water. Honestly, two steps in and I set sail. Talk about a drop-off. Luckily the water was beautifully warm. All was well as I glided around and Geoffrey swam, until a particularly large swell lifted me and the pineapple right up and dumped me unceremoniously, splat, on the rocky shore. There I lay cast in a pineapple, floundering like a beached whale. Getting to my feet wasn't easy in a landlocked pineapple but I finally got my lower limbs in order and waited for the next swell to take me back to sea.

Making it back to shore was no easier. With my feet sinking in the loose shale, it was like being encased in concrete. Geoffrey heaved the pineapple and me up the slope one foot at a time, my convulsive laughter leaving my legs like jelly; they didn't seem able to cooperate. Over the top of their designer sunglasses, the tanned and toned Italians looked on with a sense of disgust and amusement. I was pleased to note that it wasn't just us looking like idiotic simpletons as I saw a young woman exit the water by crawling out on her hands and knees. It would seem there was no easy answer.

---

1. A 1980s BBC television sitcom set in a fictional holiday camp.

GEOFFREY SPITS THE DUMMY AND SASSY GOES INTO A SULK

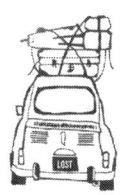

You may enter Tropea but you can't leave. A beautiful, sunny day dawned. Breakfast was a massive spread of leftover platters from the big, southern-Italian christening party. We bit into our breakfast pastries to find them liberally soaked in alcohol, a full shot in every mouthful. I paused briefly, caught off guard by this unexpected breakfast offering, then decided, oh well, if that's how they roll around here, I'll go with it. I munched on, thinking the taste set the coffee off quite nicely. I headed back to the buffet for more. *Could catch on, I guess.*

After we'd said farewell to Jenny and Nonna, we hopped in the car and attempted to programme Sassy. The day immediately started to unravel. We wanted to go back to the autoroute via the main road then travel south. But Sassy had other ideas and had plotted a very intricate path for us, heading directly cross-country for Sicily via the straightest route and conveniently ignoring all main roads. Geoffrey started to grumble but I was still happy after my alcoholic breakfast. We checked Sassy was set to motorways—tick; main roads—tick. Geoffrey tried different ways to coax her into taking us via proper roads. She steadfastly refused.

'Damn you, Sassy; you're an evil witch,' he shouted.

Nonna looked up. Geoffrey slammed Cedric into reverse and we were off.

We didn't know the way so were forced to follow Sassy's stupid trail. The first route she took us on out of Tropea was a pothole-ridden death trap heading up a mountain and ended in concrete barricades across the road (with good reason). We were forced to turn back. Sassy was furious and strongly urged us to do a U-turn then directed us to head sharp left over the cliff and into the sea. We ignored her. She got louder and commanded us to go over the cliff. Our satnav appeared to be possessed by an evil spirit. We decided to look for the green autoroute signs and follow them to the highway ourselves. We figured Sassy would give up her nonsense and reprogramme herself onto the main roads but like Nonna, she was no quitter and continued to bleat away in the background. Signs pointing to the autoroute naturally petered out to nothing and disappeared. We were fast losing time, retracing our steps, desperate to get out of Tropea.

We stopped for petrol (still in the vicinity of Tropea as we hadn't got far). It was a large petrol station with multiple bays and a uniformed worker was on the forecourt. As Geoffrey went to put the petrol in, he ran over waving and shouted, 'No petrol, no petrol.' The way this day was shaping up, we weren't surprised to hear that fuel was off the menu apparently.

We gave up trying to follow the signposts. It was getting late and we were booked on a ferry to Sicily at 12:40. The port was only an hour and a half away from Tropea. We should've had plenty of time. How hard could it be to get out of this town?

So it was back to Sassy. She was smugly pleased that we'd decided to obey her but continued to refuse to take us to the autoroute. What choice did we have? We resumed following her futile commands and ten minutes later we were in a corn field, on a track leading through a farm, naturally unpaved. The inevitable happened. Geoffrey lost the plot, savagely cursing at our possessed satnav. The tension was high as I watched the minutes tick by as we tried to get out of this endless nightmare. My alcoholic stupor was now just a distant memory. Sassy was abruptly decommissioned, although to be fair, she was lucky she wasn't ripped out and tossed among the corn.

We turned around and drove aimlessly until we chanced upon the correct road that headed to the autoroute. The tides of fortune were now in our favour. This was confirmed when we were permitted to purchase fuel from a petrol station. While there we stopped for a quick coffee. As we walked towards the café, a crowd was forming. An Italian guy called us over to look at what was happening.

'I lived in New York,' he said, 'so I know how to win.'

A crowd of Italian, swarthy, shifty-looking types was gathered around a little table, with the classic 'three cups and a dice hidden underneath' scenario.

'Look, look,' said the supposed New York guy (whose job was to draw in the targets). 'He's a tourist and winning,' he proclaimed, neglecting the fact that not one of the gathered men looked remotely like a tourist. He suddenly decided to play and said, 'Help me, help me,' directing us both to put a finger on a cup, which we stupidly did without thinking. All the men began their role, talking fast and loudly and trying to confuse us (not hard at the best of times), waving loads of cash in our faces. The New York guy shouted to us, 'You've already won, quick, all you have to do is open your wallets and show them your money.'

'Yeah right,' I declared with a roll of my eyes. 'It's a scam and I'm off for my coffee,' and I walked away. I suddenly realised Geoffrey wasn't with me, looked back and the damned fool had his wallet open, showing them his cash. 'GEOFFREYYYYY,' I shouted, 'it's a scam. Close your wallet.' *Local Mafia perhaps?* I thought. That night I showed him on YouTube the 31 top scams in Italy; this rest-area scam was right up there.

Once we were back on the correct route, Sassy was recommissioned to direct us onto the autoroute but the little madam was in a strop because we hadn't followed her advice so she just refused to speak to us; point-blank refused and sat in a sulky silence. We had the screen map so I just had to call out which way to go until Sassy finally got over herself and did what she was flipping well meant to do. She suddenly recognised there was an autoroute and decided we were a lost cause so she would take us that way, like it was all her idea. I made a mental note to Google 'demonic possession of satnavs'. So that was the entire morning gone, just to travel about 30 kilometres. And off we went onto the autoroute at last with barely enough time to get to the ferry. If all went well, we would have twenty minutes to spare; 'if' being the operative word.

We arrived at the exit for Villa San Giovanni. All we had to do now was exit at the right point for the Caronte ferry but unsurprisingly we took a wrong turn on a complicated loop-de-loop and couldn't get back. We now found ourselves stuck fast in a chaotic melee of mad Italians, looking for creative ways through one big traffic jam. My heart slumped; there was no way we were going to make that ferry. I sighed heavily.

It was tense in the car; total silence. I didn't dare say a word as Geoffrey looked like he was on a knife's edge and about to lose it again. He pulled out of the traffic to go in the opposite direction, away from the congested port, before stopping at the side of the road to count to ten and breathe. We now had five minutes to make our ferry. Drawing on Nonna's no-quit attitude, Geoffrey instructed Sassy to get us to the port pronto and lo and behold the little madam did as instructed. We had our doubts about where she was taking us as it didn't appear to be an obvious route. But suddenly, voilà, a sign appeared, pointing to the Caronte car ferry. We screeched onto the dock with Geoffrey shouting at me, 'Which way? Which way?'

'Left, left,' I shouted while he was shouting, 'Where? Where?'

'Where I'm pointing,' I yelled back and with that we squealed to a halt on the dock. Geoffrey grabbed the voucher which needed to be exchanged for a ticket and sprinted off. The ferry was pulling in and the other cars started their engines.

Oh shit, I thought. *I'm going to be left here in the car lane with all the Italians honking their horns at me.* Suddenly a gypsy appeared, looking in the window at me and demanding money. I hit the auto door-lock button. *That's all I flipping well need.* With no time to spare, a hot and sweaty Geoffrey came lolloping along the dock, leapt in, gunned the engines and we were off onto the ferry. In typical Italian style, there was no need to drive on in any sort of systematic way; all three lanes just took off for the boat in a giant free-for-all. We needn't have bothered with the ticket either as no one checked we had one.

Most people elected to stay in their cars for the twenty-minute crossing to Sicily. Apart from our quick petrol stop, we'd been stuck in that car and lost since 9:30 so we sprinted upstairs to use the loo, grabbed a panini then raced back to the car to wolf it down and swallow some water before we drove off the ferry.

Alas our woes weren't over as Sassy once again refused to speak to us. She was disorientated by the ferry crossing and had our location set in the middle of the ocean so we left her to sort herself out and faced the mayhem of Messina port and city alone. To our utter disbelief that anything else could possibly go wrong, Cedric was stuffed. He now had about as much oomph as a dying flea and it was obvious we'd been sold dodgy petrol. This only compounded all Geoffrey's fears about the Mafia and reservations about coming to Sicily.

The car could no longer head up a slope, which was one gigantic issue as we had to go straight up a steep hill to get out of the port and onto the autoroute. Cedric could only move in first gear with the engine revving and roaring loudly as we lurched slowly up through the bedlam with Geoffrey shouting at poor Cedric and Sassy no doubt laughing. I held my breath. As I looked around, it all seemed very disordered and unruly; a bit on the rough side. I hoped Geoffrey wasn't right about Sicily.

Cars and people were doing whatever they wanted to do; chaos ruled. And through it all crept Cedric, who could now only move at the pace of a snail while impatient Sicilian drivers made their feelings very clear.

'I don't believe it,' shouted Geoffrey. We were nearly at our exit but an old man had set up a stall selling chestnuts on the road, in our lane. 'Oh for God's sake,' yelled Geoffrey. 'Now I've got to try and go around the old fart.' I sighed deeply. 'Take your chestnuts and f#@% off,' shouted Geoffrey. 'Whose stupid idea was it to come to Sicily?'

Eventually we made it out of Messina port alive and stayed on the pretty much flat autoroute for two and a half hours via very high viaducts and tunnels until we turned off at Cefalù. Two kilometres up the road inland was our closest village, Campofelice di Roccella, where we stopped to try and get groceries so we could have dinner. An enormous supermarket and 3:30 p.m. on a Tuesday and it was shut as it was siesta time and the Italians needed to go home for a nap, which was all well and good unless you were the ones standing despondently in the car park staring in the window. Feeling defeated by the whole day, we carried on, jerking our way up a steep hill in first gear to our villa where we rang the owner and waited for the big, electronic gates to open. Cedric was too busy half-heartedly wheel-spinning in a pothole to make it through when the gates opened. We watched in dismay as they closed again. More sighs. The owner (also probably sighing) then had to get in his car and come down the drive to see why the idiot foreigners didn't come through the gate. He re-opened them and Cedric managed to get his daft self out of the hole and follow him up to the villa.

The day improved markedly when we saw an amazing villa set in sumptuous gardens complete with a magnificent, sparkling blue pool. Francesco didn't speak English but showed us around and we said '*Sì*' a lot, despite not having a clue what he was saying. Bluff it out and nod a lot, I say. But I did manage to tell him he had a *bella casa* (beautiful house). We popped back down to the supermarket once the Italians were awake again then I cooked a dinner of pasta and salad which we ate out on the terrace while Geoffrey had a well-deserved *vino rosso* (red wine).

We'd booked the villa last minute a week before after another had been cancelled so it was a little more pricey, but wow, we had a pool and views down over the coast to the sea and the weather was hot. We could even see the two plumes of smoke across the water coming from the volcanic islands of Stromboli and Vulcano. Geoffrey declared that next day would be a rest day and he wasn't going near Cedric. I agreed and so there we were: the pineapple was inflated; we'd swum already; Geoffrey was poolside and I was typing. We were keeping a wary eye out for scorpions around the paving too as there was lots of bug life with lizards, millipedes and butterflies.

It was almost time for the pool again but first, now that we had Wi-Fi, I needed to Google 'demonic possession of satnavs'.

Ciao.

DRIVING OVER A LANDSLIP

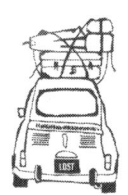

A week later and it was arrivederci to Sicily. It had come as an unexpected pleasure and blew away Geoffrey's misconceptions. He was convinced we would be encased in concrete by the Mafia or at the very least have our tyres slashed and be robbed of all our possessions. He had a vision in his mind of shady men in dark suits lurking in the shadows, guns at the ready. He was delighted to report that he loved Sicily and would happily return. The biggest revelation was the people, who were genuinely warm, relaxed, friendly and welcoming. We never felt unsafe at any point; I would be more worried about crime in Rome, Florence or Venice than Sicily.

On our last day, Francesco, his wife, Sophia, and her friend Giulia arrived at the villa to see us off. None of them could speak English so Francesco's wife used her phone translator to tell us she hoped we had a good vacation and added that they got quite a few Germans. I looked puzzled and said in what was probably extremely poor Italian, '*Non German, sono Nuova Zelanda.*' There was a horrified gasp as she turned to Francesco, shouted at him in Italian and gave him a good whack, yelling what amounted to 'you told me they were Germans; we've had highly prized New Zealanders under our roof all this time and we never knew, you fool' then she whacked him again for good measure.

We were immediately taken in hand and whisked inside and away from the car. They weren't letting us get away that easily. With that, the excited inquisition began. I got out my phone app but trying to talk into it while three animated Italians were all jabbering away at once wasn't very successful as it kept picking up the background chatter of the lively conversations. Giulia kept repeating, 'Twenty hours fly, mamma mia, mamma mia.' Francesco meanwhile was interrogating Geoffrey on why we had a car with French plates. Geoffrey told him we'd stolen the car, which was no help at all.

Sophia asked via her phone app where we'd been. With the app failing, I resorted to mime and was forced to hold my arms out and make like an aeroplane, then say Milano. Then I held a pretend steering wheel like I was driving and said Venezia, followed by the other destinations we'd visited, all to many gasps. The next question was how long we'd been on holiday. I was stumped. I had no idea how to say seven weeks in Italian so resorted to finger-counting. More gasps. Lastly Sophia asked did we like Sicily. That one was easy. '*Sì, molto bene, bella, bella, bella.*' (Very good, beautiful, beautiful, beautiful.) And with that we took our leave to a chorus of arrivedercis but not before Francesco had quickly cut some of his roses to hand to me through the car window.

To leave Sicily we had to return via the port of Messina where a typical Italian Carabinieri was on point duty in the middle of a large intersection; it was classic Italy at its best. There was no false attempt at professionalism. He became so angry at the traffic's stupidity that he turned bright red in the face and had steam coming off his head, yelling at cars and dramatically throwing his arms around, all while attempting to carry out a shouted conversation with a friend on the pavement. While distracted with his private chat, he accidentally waved a horse carriage full of cruise-ship passengers through the intersection, forgot about them and waved a bus through from the opposite direction. The bus naturally paused as there was a horse carriage in the way but the Carabiniere had his back to the carriage and became incensed at the bus driver, yelling and gesticulating at him to 'MOVE IT, pronto pronto'. Turning, he saw the carriage, realised his error, responded with a typical 'oh well' shrug, turned away and carried on.

One particularly bold driver dared to do the unthinkable and pulled into the intersection, blocking other cars from getting through. Well that was the last straw. With sweat dripping off the Carabiniere, his arms waved faster than a rotor blade and Italian oaths filled the air. We didn't understand the Italian but we got the gist of it. He appeared to be threatening the driver with an early death if he didn't get out of the way pronto, pronto.

Surprisingly we managed to find our way to the ferry easily this time and approached the ticket counter with our voucher to exchange for the tickets.

'But where is your ticket?' the attendant enquired.

Geoffrey and I looked at each other. What ticket? Surely we just redeemed this voucher which was proof of purchase and had worked beautifully on the way over. But no, apparently we were meant to keep the ticket from the journey over as it was also our return ticket. Bugger. Geoffrey mimed screwing up a bit of paper and dramatically throwing it in a bin.

'Oh no, no, no, oh mamma mia, mamma mia,' the man said in horror, slapping his hands to his cheeks. 'Without this you cannot sail. It is the rules.'

Our eyes widened in alarm. Were we trapped in Sicily? A lady behind us with better English helped us to understand. We now needed to purchase a new return ticket and pay again, despite holding a voucher and receipt for payment in our hands. *Oh Lordy. There go the rest of our euros.*

After paying for the ferry twice, Geoffrey was a bit grumbly as we exited the ferry and set Sassy to guide us to Tropea for the night. You may remember the trouble we had getting out of Tropea. Well let me tell you, it's no better getting in. Cedric, who after a tankful of proper petrol was thankfully no longer playing up, bravely exited the autoroute bound for Tropea...straight onto an overgrown track.

This can't be right, we thought, but double-checking with Sassy confirmed that we were indeed at the correct exit. There were no other cars around. How strange. Undaunted we blindly carried on, not noticing the barriers that had been pushed to one side. Our suspicions about this no longer being an actual road began to increase along with a sense of unease. Cedric stoically bounced through the rutted, potholed track bordered by overgrown bulrushes on both sides. We were forced to drive on the wrong side of the road as Geoffrey's side appeared to be getting swallowed whole by a forest of bullrushes oozing on a slow but steady course downhill. A pattern became self-evident; we were driving on one giant landslip.

On our left, the land above was steadily encroaching across the other lane, creating regular landslips to navigate around. Meanwhile my side was visibly slumped on an angle, tilting over the side of the hill. Our suspicions were confirmed when we came around the corner to find what was left of the road split in two, with Geoffrey's side being a foot higher than mine. Cedric paused. We just looked at the road. I sighed heavily (again) and Geoffrey seemed to be thinking 'oh well, in for a penny in for a pound'. He positioned his side's two wheels on the upper piece of road and my side's wheels on the lower section of the vertical split, and off we went, driving along on a lean like two lunatics. There was nothing for it but to laugh, and laugh we did. We looked utterly ridiculous driving at a 45-degree angle. Nine flipping kilometres we drove like this; mental.

Eventually we arrived at the end of the road to find there were indeed barriers but someone had kindly moved them aside. We could only shake our heads and sigh. Geoffrey's earlier good humour came to an abrupt end as Sassy infuriated him by directing Cedric up farm tracks and driveways, following one dead end after another until eventually we got to Tropea quite by accident and not due to Sassy's diligence. By some wondrous miracle, we found our location was only about a kilometre from our B&B. The gods were truly shining on us at last. *Good*, I thought as I looked in my handbag for our check-in paperwork in anticipation of our imminent arrival. *What a relief*.

But Sassy hadn't finished with us yet. She decided to test Geoffrey's blood pressure a little more and she certainly succeeded in getting it to boiling point. She confidently led us down a very steep, cobbled lane that narrowed considerably as we went until it was barely wide enough for the car to get through and certainly not wide enough even to attempt to turn back. We were stuck, constricted, much like the veins now protruding from Geoffrey's forehead. He stopped the car and went ballistic at Sassy, yelling at her and stabbing at her screen in an attempt to inflict mortal wounds upon her for her stupidity. Me laughing like a nervous hyena didn't help matters much either.

'What are we going to do now?' snapped Geoffrey.

Bonnie Tyler singing 'Holding out for a Hero' sprang to mind but as I looked around, only two bored old nonnas were watching us from a bench. *Hmmm, time for the backup plan.* I whipped out my phone. The previous evening I'd downloaded the route to my phone app, not trusting Sassy. Geoffrey's face lit up. He was able to look at it and figure out not only where we were but which of the alleys were one way and which route would lead us out of this maze and back to safety. Praise the Lord, it worked and we were very relieved to find our B&B for the night. Geoffrey needed a lie down and a gin and Sassy needed a swift kick up the bum.

When Geoffrey had returned to a calmer state of mind, we ventured into the old town for dinner at a trattoria. Once seated, we opened our menus to see what gastronomic delights awaited us. Geoffrey suddenly let out a loud guffaw. 'Look, look what's on the flippin' menu. Only pulped hedgehogs. Unbelievable!' Oh my God, we doubled up laughing, plagued by heinous visions of hedgehogs rammed inside blenders. Geoffrey photographed the menu as proof. 'No one will believe us otherwise,' he said.

After a very non-hedgehoggy meal of pasta, we followed a noise that had accompanied our dinner to see what was happening. It led us directly into the town square, packed with locals gazing up at a brightly lit balcony above us. There were giant banners strung across the tower where a selection of prospective mayoral candidates were making speeches in Italian about what they would do for Tropea.

'Well you can start with the flipping roads,' muttered Geoffrey. We wondered how many of the candidates were affiliated with the local Mafia who were a massive problem in the area.

The next day we arrived on the Amalfi coast for three nights before we said farewell to Italy after a 6,000-kilometre journey and headed to Oman for the last week of our seven-week adventure. Oman, where it's hot and dry. Oh, but wait, what had just appeared on my news feed? Only that a very unusual cyclone had hit the country. Flooding was expected to continue until our arrival. The news clip held wonderfully evocative footage of camels swimming for their lives across flood waters and entire villages surrounded by a sea of mud. *I do apologise, Oman, but it would seem our imminent arrival and perpetual bad luck has caused this strange anomaly in your weather.*

On the plus side, it was with great relief that we logged onto the laptop to find the Royal Oman Police had granted our visas. Furthermore our Amalfi apartment kindly printed them out for us as we had no access to a printer. So it seemed with papers all in order, we were cleared to go to the land of the swimming camel.

Buona sera (good night) from Amalfi.

GOATS AND GIZZARDS

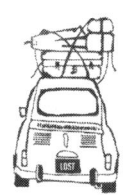

*A*s we sat at our gate at the Emirates terminal in Dubai Airport, I felt like the clock was ticking too fast. Suddenly our seven-week solo adventure was nearing an end as we had just one week left. While we waited to board our flight to Oman, I nervously checked the weather and news updates for Muscat. Thankfully the medicane had moved out to sea and the flash flooding was over. It was autumn in Oman, though maybe that's not even a thing there. It's just flipping hot or less flipping hot.

Given that I can't stand the heat, you may wonder why I chose to go to Oman. Most people think of the Middle East and shy away nervously but a *Travel Guides* episode where they visited Oman had piqued my interest. I did a bit of research and what I read sealed the deal. The consensus was that it was a peaceful nation with a much-loved leader at that time, Sultan Qaboos, who was held in high regard by the people. The Omanis are tolerant of all religions and very welcoming to any tourists who come their way. They're not at war with anyone; in fact Sultan Qaboos acted as a peaceful mediator between the other Gulf neighbours. Oman also has a low crime rate and I wondered if this was due to no alcohol. Decision made, I packed my array of fans and told Geoffrey where we were going after I booked it, much like Venice and Sicily. The less he knew, the less he had to worry about.

After a short flight from Dubai, Geoffrey and I arrived at Muscat International Airport, one of us full of excitement, the other thinking 'why have I been dragged here against my will?' The reluctant one was pleasantly surprised with the warm Omani welcome we received at the airport. At the sight of our New Zealand passports, they whisked us through long queues and made us feel like VIPs. Even the car rental went smoothly with the staff full of genuine interest to meet Kiwis, giving us smiles and handshakes. Geoffrey became suspicious; things didn't normally go this well.

We headed off into the hazy, 35-degree heat, following Sultan Qaboos Street towards our destination of Sidab Beach, 55 kilometres away, where we were to stay with a local Omani family in their house; accommodation I'd found on Airbnb. This was quite a stretch for Geoffrey to cope with, being landed in a foreign environment on the Arabian Peninsula, an entirely alien culture, and now expected to live with strangers for a week. To say he thought I'd lost my mind was an understatement.

One of us was immediately seduced by the magnificently manicured, tree-lined boulevards with sumptuous gardens, stately buildings, mosques, ornate golden statues and pastel-hued, Arabian-style mansions. This one was also not really paying attention to navigating; she was entranced and euphoric at such wondrously different surroundings. Eyes wide and a grin on her face, she admired the decorative Arabic architecture and mesmerisingly bejewelled mosque towers in tones of sapphire and white against a crisp blue sky.

Geoffrey's suspicions were confirmed when an hour later we arrived back at Muscat International Airport after doing one giant loop and returning via the Muscat freeway. I was reluctantly brought back to reality and forced to focus on navigating by Geoffrey's apoplectic outburst at the sight of all the aeroplanes once again. The 130-kilometres-per-hour speed limit made him even more jittery as did the amount of large, black, four-wheel-drive vehicles hot on his tail.

I called on the travel angels to intervene and by pure chance rather than any navigational skills (because truthfully I still wasn't paying attention), we happened to arrive at the right house in the right fishing village. Even Geoffrey was stunned and waited for me to get cautiously out of the car and approach the door. As I did I was hit by a wall of all-enveloping heat after the cool of the car's interior.

Geoffrey was warily watching the curious locals who were appearing to stare at us. As I knocked at the door, one of the Omani gentlemen stepped forward and asked if he could help. I explained we were looking for Najeeb as we were coming to stay in the house. He grinned broadly and said that he'd just gone to collect his girls from school. He rang Najeeb then said we were to let ourselves in, third floor and first door on the left.

We crept up the tiled stairs, feeling very much like we shouldn't be entering a stranger's house.

'What if it's a trap?' suggested Geoffrey, his suspicions returning. 'We could be locked up and our body parts sold on the black market for all we know.'

'Shut up,' I snapped. 'You're being ridiculous.'

I opened the door to the apartment. The interior was all tiled floors, patterned tiles on walls and coloured glass leading onto a balcony. Our room was a simple double room with a basin in one corner, a toilet and shower attached. The kitchen held only very basic cooking facilities, with just a portable, camping-size, two-burner gas stove on the bench, a fridge and further benches. It was sweltering in the kitchen with just a ceiling fan for cooling.

Najeeb and the girls appeared to have their own rooms but there was no lounge of any sort, just the small balcony with a glass table and some chairs which looked across at Sidab Beach as the accommodation was just two houses back from the Arabian Sea.

As we glanced out at our surroundings, we saw we were in a small bay with a village of traditional adobe buildings in colours of terracotta, caramel, blue and white. The bay was framed by tall, steep, dusty, golden cliffs.

Once we'd investigated our new abode and dragged all our luggage up the stairs, we nervously went in search of a shop to buy groceries and water. A herd of goats lazily meandered the streets, tugging at the odd piece of vegetation or scraggly weeds. It was only a small town so it didn't take us long to find the little grocery store. It was lunchtime and everything appeared closed. We were puzzled as there were cars out the front of the little shop but big shutters were pulled down, covering whatever was sold within. Later we found out this was just to keep the sun out.

We stopped and watched, puzzled as to what to do, until we saw someone come out of the shop and some school children go in. I looked at Geoffrey.

'Don't look at me,' he said. 'This was all your idea.'

I groaned. 'Come on then. Let's have a look.'

We opened the door into a tiny, dark, hot and cramped space, filled head to toe with exotic-looking grocery items. We squeezed our way down the narrow aisle and grabbed a few things which looked vaguely familiar. The meat freezer held bags of chicken gizzards and whole chickens' heads. Geoffrey took one look and decided he didn't need meat.

We could hear Arabic being spoken all around us but I'd read that English was widely understood. When we reached the counter, the gentleman totted everything up in his head as there was no till then announced that we owed him what sounded to me like vast sums of Omani baisa. He noticed our gasps of horror and looks of bewilderment. Geoffrey wisely held out some notes and the gentleman took what turned out to be about $8.

When we stepped back into the glaring sunlight and midday heat, a car screeched to a halt and a man called out, 'Hi, Denise. Hi, Geoffrey.' It was Najeeb and his teenage daughters, Maha and Aaleyah. As the only foreigners in town, we were pretty easy to spot. We joined them back at the house for a traditional Omani welcome of Turkish coffee, dates and nuts, sitting on the balcony catching the sea breeze while we got acquainted. We discovered that school was from 7:30 a.m. until 1 p.m. due to the heat. Najeeb soon headed back to his office in the nearby town of Ruwi while the girls went to their rooms to do their homework.

We decided to head to the beach so Geoffrey inflated the pineapple ready for a dip in the Gulf of Oman. We made sure we were respectfully clothed in rash tops and board shorts but we needn't have worried as the giant pineapple seemed to be the main interest, causing a few gaping mouths as we carried it conspicuously down the street and into the water. Oh, the warm, warm water, but deliciously cooling compared to the air temperature. While we floated and looked around, we were able to admire the caramel- and coffee-toned cliffs on either side of the narrow valley, bereft of any vegetation. The cliffs jutted out into the sea either side of us, forming a frame for the village of Sidab between its enclosed embrace.

Fishermen on the shore tended to their nets on the small wooden craft. Najeeb told us they fished at night, returning in the morning to sort their catch in the hot morning sun before going home to sleep. The wild cats were gathered, waiting hopefully for some scraps. Some of the fishermen earned a few extra rials by acting as water taxis for expats and tourists who wanted to be taken around to secluded private beaches for the day.

After our swim we retired for a siesta. Too hot to do anything else, we drifted off to the sound of water. Not the gently lapping waves upon the shore though; this water was rather closer than that. We had a dripping air con; well, not really dripping, more of a cascading, relentless, annoying waterfall splashing all over the floor. What were we to do? We only had two towels; the family were so nice so we didn't want to appear whiny. I emptied the rubbish bin and placed it underneath. The noise volume increased to a steady plop, plop, dribble, drop followed by an intermittent pssssshhhhh.

For dinner that night, Najeeb offered to cook for us but not wanting to be a burden, we rustled up a gourmet meal of our two-minute noodles followed by beans on toast, which was all that we'd found in the corner store that looked vaguely familiar. Najeeb looked horrified. He liked to cook, although this was frowned upon by the local men as it's traditionally considered women's work. He deftly produced flatbreads to have with homemade hummus and goat's cheese, lettuce and tomato. I looked longingly at it. Geoffrey made us a cup of tea and poured in the milk we thought we'd purchased. Gluggy, clotted lumps of yogurt plopped into our cups. We stared at it in horror and tipped it out. Najeeb made us some Turkish coffee.

Hearing the sound of cars going past, tooting and voices raised in greeting, Najeeb and the girls called us to join them on the balcony to observe the evening ritual. In Sidab the residents gather as the sun lowers and cools. Tooting of horns is commonplace as the villagers greet each other and stop for a chat. Najeeb's girls looked longingly at the Westerners and children swimming at the beach. As adolescent females they were unable to bathe publicly.

While we caught the evening breeze and watched village life below, we heard anecdotes about the village and its characters from Najeeb and of Omani school life from the girls. We didn't want to pry but gathered that Najeeb and his wife had parted company amicably a few years back. Najeeb told us about his friend from North Africa who believed in jinns—Islamic spirits that can be good or evil and are thought to take up residence sometimes in houses, making mischief and trouble for the occupants. Village life here was still steeped in age-old beliefs and superstitions woven into daily life. Najeeb, Maha and Aaleyah asked lots of questions about life in New Zealand. No topics were off limits and we learnt a little about the Muslim faith and listened spellbound as the evening call to prayer echoed its haunting melody, waxing and waning through the warm, still evening.

As we retired to our room for the night, I had a wash at the basin in our bedroom then pulled the plug out, horrified as the water poured all over my feet. I stared down at the mess now soaking into the bedside mat, grabbing one of our two towels to stem the tide. We now had one towel between us but we wanted to fit in; we wanted to be liked. *It's hot; we have one pillow each, one towel to share, a free-flowing basin and our air con sounds like Niagara Falls, but we will* not *complain.* Overnight I discreetly dried the carpet and towel on the balcony and planned to ask Najeeb innocently for a couple more towels next day.

Over the top of the ever-present drip, we listened to Sidab's night sounds. The cats gathered on the beach, scrounging for food or meowing plaintively under balconies; the sound of cat fights rang out around the beach. A full moon rose over the bay; a goat bleated nearby and the rubbish rustled as the goat invaded the neighbours' bins unseen. Some of the village women had put dishes of leftovers on their doorsteps where the cats or goats would find them. Silence fell in Sidab apart from the ever-present crickets as the moon rose higher in the night sky. The large crabs that lived in deep tunnels in the sand came out and scuttled sideways across the sandy beach, stalked by playful cats. The village rested until the sun rose on another day.

Najeeb had explained to us the night before that breakfast was included in the price and he would leave it out for us as he and the girls left about 7 a.m. for work and school. We slept late and appeared in the kitchen about 10 a.m., expecting some bread or cereal. He'd laid out on the bench a plate of boiled eggs, a strange type of fritter with something black in it, goat's cheese, a decidedly over-ripe mango, cucumber, dates and *laban* (which means sour milk in Arabic), a salty drink made of yogurt and buttermilk. It had been sitting in an un-air-conditioned kitchen in the heat for three hours. Our fault for sleeping in. Geoffrey and I peered at the offering closely. What should we do? We couldn't appear ungrateful so we either had to eat it or hide it.

'The cats,' I called out triumphantly. 'We'll feed it to the cats below the balcony.'

We ate more beans and noodles.

Geoffrey and I headed to the historic Mutrah Souk, parking along the famous Muscat Corniche. He couldn't fathom the strange parking-meter machines but no tanties were needed here. We only had to look confused and a local would swoop to the rescue, asking if they could help. Couldn't find the entrance to the souk? No problem, an exotically dressed Omani came to the rescue.

The souk is famous for selling gold, frankincense and myrrh, all in one location. There were no tourists around, just Geoffrey and me, so we were prime targets. It only took one shop for Geoffrey to be trounced up like a chicken, dressed head to toe in the traditional round cap (called a kumma) and a white dishdasha robe, complete with complimentary tassel. All he did was follow me into a shop and suddenly he looked like a prize twit. I found it hard to control my mirth and whipped out the camera for a photo.

To appease his lordship, we entered a coffee shop. The locals took one look at us and stood up, insisting we take their table. Geoffrey was perplexed. Things were just too easy in Oman; this was unbalancing his equilibrium.

'What should we have to eat?' I pondered, then discovered that every coffee shop sells only one type of food, each specialising in something different. This one sold little savoury stuffed pastries which tasted good.

On the way home, we found a large supermarket and managed to buy a few more recognisable items. It was still swelteringly hot so after a quick cuppa and some melon we sauntered across the road with the giant pineapple, many eyes following us.

That evening Najeeb showed me how to make homemade hummus and we joined him and the girls for dinner on the balcony. The food was more in tune with the climate: deliciously soft wraps filled with the fresh hummus, tomatoes, cucumber and lettuce. Najeeb and Geoffrey stayed up late talking on the balcony, sipping Turkish coffee and snacking on dates while they discussed their lives, the similarities and differences. I lay in bed listening to the steady dribble, drip, plop of the air con, the kittens meowing, goats foraging and the ever-present crickets chirping.

HOT STUFF

*O*ver the next few days, Geoffrey and I explored some of the local fortresses dating from the 9th century, including Nizwa, Oman's largest.

The large main tower at Nizwa fort contained many gruesome defence mechanisms, such as holes where boiling date syrup could be poured onto enemy heads. It was about an hour inland from Muscat where temperatures were soaring to about 45 degrees. There was a huge, cylindrical courtyard at the top of the tower with massive stone walls dotted with arrow slits and steps leading up to the top of the ramparts at regular intervals around the cylinder.

The sun beat down; the stone-daubed walls baked in the hot sun. At the top of each set of stairs, we could gaze down upon the scenery below. Geoffrey was intent upon climbing them all but I'd had enough. I climbed partway up the set of stairs in the shadow of the wall and slowly slithered to the ground on my sweat-soaked bottom. I rummaged in my handbag and out came my battery-powered hand fan. I held it up to my beet-red face, a mere inch from my nose as I wafted the moving air around. I was sapped, hair plastered to my head, limp and damp.

I watched Geoffrey, who was in heaven, bouncing around these massive forts like a mountain goat. I disliked him intensely from my hot stone step. I was done. I'd sweated where I didn't know sweat could be. Not even battery fan and Singapore fan combined could fix this one and I longed for the cool interior of the air-conditioned car.

'I'm all fortressed out,' I said to Geoffrey when he returned.

'Let's head back towards Muscat.'

'I've never seen anything like this before in my life,' I exclaimed to him as we drove.

The wide valley we were following was dry and arid, dotted with frankincense trees and surrounded by the chocolate-toned, rocky hills, coloured by the magnesite minerals within. At regular intervals we passed small towns and villages of white-daubed and pastel-hued homes built in the traditional style of mud-brick houses. The villages were marked by the presence of date-palm plantations, the greenness of which was in stark contrast to the surrounding golden desert tones. The coolness of the car revived me.

'Camels!' I screamed. 'Stop the car, Geoffrey.'

And I was off, suddenly infused with energy as I leapt from the car and charged off after two camels. Geoffrey was left looking dazed, waiting patiently while I went camel-bothering.

When I got back in the car, I must have unwittingly let a fly in with me. As we drove along, I read aloud to Geoffrey from the guide book, telling him how many species of snakes and scorpions there were in Oman. Two minutes later something tickled my arm and I let out a blood-curdling scream.

Geoffrey shouted, 'What is it?'

I saw the fly land on Geoffrey's stomach and walloped him hard in the belly with the guide book.

He yelled.

'It's just a fly,' I commented. If looks could kill!

We pulled in at Marina Bandar Al Rowdha to book a sunset cruise on one of the traditional wooden Omani dhows. I stepped out of the car to walk the 50 metres or so to the marina office. Geoffrey got out and went to lock the door but I hopped straight back in and wailed, 'I can't do it.'

Geoffrey returned to the car and looked at me as if I'd finally lost the plot. 'Do what?' he asked.

'Turn the air con on,' I practically screamed. 'I can't do it. I'm not walking over there; it's too hot.'

Geoffrey looked flummoxed as he gazed across at the marina office. 'It's just over there,' he shouted. 'What are you talking about, woman?'

'I don't care. I'm not walking another step. Take me home,' I wailed.

'You're demented, woman,' he grumbled and off we went in silence; well, silent except for the delightful, steady whirring of the air con on full.

ONE WAY ▶

The next day we explored the Sultan Qaboos Grand Mosque and the National Museum of Muscat. I'd read online that they were air conditioned. Once a guard had checked we were respectfully clothed, we were welcomed into the marble courtyard where we followed a symmetrically laid-out pattern of fountains and garden up to the entrance to the mosque to stow our shoes in a locker before entering through gigantic, arched wooden doors. The Grand Mosque was truly magnificent; the Arabic architecture, colourful tiles, arches, domes, carpets and chandeliers were not to be missed. A guide pointed out that the carpets in the main men's mosque were patterned and had no lines because men knew how to stand in a straight line, whereas the women's prayer room had lines on the carpet as women hadn't mastered this skill. I found this very funny but given the hushed environment we were in, I wisely kept quiet.

Geoffrey was all swotty at the museum, reading all the displays and studying everything carefully. He asked me afterwards, 'What did you enjoy?'

'The air con, the loo with toilet paper and the iced coffee.'

He rolled his eyes and called me a peasant.

After my meltdown at the marina the previous day, I'd booked the sunset dhow cruise online. So off we went to the marina in the cooler part of the evening and set sail on a wooden dhow straight off the pages of Sinbad the Sailor, lying back on sumptuous, patterned cushions, eating dates and nuts and drinking coffee. The Arabian Sea was like waves of silk, the sun a lowering, brightly burning ball on the horizon as we headed along the coast past fortresses of old and amazingly bronze-hued cliffs turning burnt amber as the sun began to set.

The highlight of the cruise was to be sailing into Sultan Qaboos Port to watch the sun go down over the historic town of Mutrah. But what was this? As we approached the port, an ominous-looking, military-grey Royal Oman Police boat came speeding out of nowhere, heading directly for us. This formidable vessel pulled alongside. We passengers looked on, watchful and alert as the police yelled something to our captain and crew in Arabic. There was much arm-waving, tension and angry voices as our captain and crew shouted back.

Cell phones were pulled out and calls made. The police boat had large, menacing, automatic weapons pointed at our dhow. Automatic weapons trumped sumptuous cushions and coffee; it was time to retreat. *Where's Sinbad when you need him?* We were unclear on the reasons behind our sudden eviction from the harbour but the intentions were clear. The police boat escorted us out, guns looming at the ready.

By this time the sun had set and we all missed it, distracted as we were by the threatening displays of power. Oh the drama. It struck me as quite bizarre to be lounging back on Arabic-style cushions enjoying a coffee and slowly chewing dates while guns were pointed at us.

'Never a dull moment,' sighed Geoffrey.

We discovered later in the news that the Israeli president had come to Oman to hold top-secret peace talks with Sultan Qaboos and was staying on the Sultan's grand motor yacht in the port. Our little cruise boat was inadvertently entering the no-go area guarding the president. Why was I not surprised?

Meanwhile Najeeb's breakfast treats continued unabated and we were now approaching the kitchen with something akin to dread each morning, afraid to see what the next offering might be. We should have said something but we didn't want to offend. The local wild cats and goats dined well that week. We felt awful but our Western stomachs just couldn't palate such exotic, unrefrigerated treats in the morning.

We did however continue to adopt the same evening meal as Najeeb and his girls, sharing with them the lovely soft flatbreads and various fillings. The girls excelled themselves one night, cooking a fresh fish from one of the local fishermen. They fried it in squares with an exotic mixture of spices and lime paired with a lovely light salsa.

On our last evening with Najeeb, Maha and Aaleyah, we wanted to cook a meal for them as a thank you for their kindness and hospitality. We prepared what we'd been eating in Sicily: spaghetti aglio e olio, with garlic, olive oil, chilli, lemon zest, parsley and the pasta water; simple but delicious. They appeared to enjoy it and were very appreciative. We all retired to the balcony one last time for the evening ritual.

The young local boys commenced their nightly game of free-wheeling on their bikes down the slope across the street that ran parallel to the beach then slowly rode back up, ready to do it again, deftly swerving around any cars or people. The local Omani men gathered, distinguished by their dress, wearing the traditional kumma and a white or sometimes brown dishdasha, the tassel on their gown perfumed with fragrant frankincense. This same group of men gathered every evening to sit on the beach, removing their leather sandals and sitting in a row on the brow of the sand, looking out across the water. There they stayed, peacefully discussing daily life.

Not far from them, the Bangladeshi men also gathered; these were mainly the hardworking people employed in lesser-paid jobs from rubbish collection to tending the grand and opulent gardens and grounds of the public gardens around the city. The men were together but separated by backgrounds and religion.

Soon the call to prayer would echo around the village. This was preceded by the Omani men getting up from where they were sitting and dispersing towards the mosque. As the call echoed eerily, permeating every corner and household in the village, the beach became the domain of the Bangladeshis, the boys and the Westerners. Some of the boys started a game of beach soccer while others floated on chilli-bin lids just off the beach, fishing. The women and girls were at home, attending to household chores, studying or preparing a late-evening meal.

The sun had dropped and the Westerners had left the beach and the evening meals had been eaten. Now that it was dark, the village women in their long, black abayas came down to the beach for a stroll, some with their daughters, all discreetly covered. They carried bags with them and disappeared to the far end of the beach where they could bathe or paddle privately, reserving their modesty and unseen by the men. It was a long, hot day for the women, who wore their abaya with pride. These few minutes at the end of each day washed away the sweat and cooled their bodies.

The week had passed so quickly and all too soon it was time for affectionate farewells to a family who had truly welcomed us into their home and provided us with an experience never to be forgotten. I wondered what sort of week we would've had at a hotel. I was sure it would've been lovely but it certainly wouldn't have given us this personal insight into daily life in Oman. We were leaving richer for the experience.

As we flew on to Dubai, I remembered how I'd felt when we'd arrived in Oman: that pit of excitement in my tummy, that feeling I only get when I'm travelling and experiencing something new and foreign to me.

I'm so overwhelmed with curiosity to see, hear, smell and taste that my senses come alive. *I* come alive. It's this feeling that's addictive; my whole being awakens to the new, the different, the exciting. This is why I travel. At home I'm restless. I know there's more out there and I want to grab it with both hands.

As I lay in our Dubai sleep pod in transit, listening to Geoffrey's rhythmic rumblings in the darkened, enclosed pod, I reflected over the seven weeks of travel. Yes, we'd survived solo travel (just) without killing each other and had had a pretty good time but part of me still longed for the possibility of future travel together as a family. I resolved to do everything in my power to make it happen. With Jan away at sea and Don living away from home and mid-science degree, it wouldn't be easy.

Never a quitter, I tried, booking a family trip to Koh Samui in December 2019. Only three of us made it as Don was awarded a valuable summer scholarship job he needed to accept.

This was to be our last overseas travel for quite some time as far away in China a virus was beginning its march across the globe unchecked. COVID-19 had grounded us. Plans for another trip to Europe, including a return to Oman, are currently on hold as New

Zealand closed its borders amid the raging pandemic sweeping the world.

What will our next adventure be? Has Geoffrey and his questionable driving been silenced for good? Only time can tell. When you ask Geoffrey where he would most like to return, he replies, 'Sicily and Oman.'

It's best I don't tell him yet where I have in mind!

MESSAGE FROM THE AUTHOR

I sincerely thank you for reading this book and I hope you enjoyed it. I'd be grateful if you could take a few minutes to leave a review on Amazon or Goodreads. I welcome Facebook friend requests and would be delighted if you followed me on Instagram too where you can see photos from my travels.

I'm happy to answer any questions you may have so do please get in touch with me by:

Email: sharon.hayhurst@xtra.co.nz
Facebook: www.facebook.com/sharon.hayhurst.3
Instagram: www.instagram.com/sharonhslm

If you enjoy reading memoirs, I recommend you pop over to the Facebook group We Love Memoirs to chat with me and other authors: www.facebook.com/groups/welovememoirs

ACKNOWLEDGEMENTS

I would like to thank Victoria Twead for her advice and Jacky Donovan for putting up with me throughout the editing process.

Printed in Great Britain
by Amazon